# The Hertfordshire Regiment
*An Illustrated History*

This book is dedicated to all those who have
contributed to the achievements of the
Hertfordshire Regiment in peace and in war,
but especially to those who fell in action
1914–1918 and 1939–1945

*Elizabeth R*

1950

HER MAJESTY QUEEN ELIZABETH
Honorary Colonel, 1st Battalion The Hertfordshire Regiment
1938–1961

# The Hertfordshire Regiment

*An Illustrated History*

Lieutenant-Colonel J. D. SAINSBURY, T.D.

**CASTLEMEAD PUBLICATIONS**
WARE

First Published 1988

CASTLEMEAD PUBLICATIONS
Swains Mill, 4A Crane Mead,
Ware, Herts, SG12 9PY
Publishing division of
WARD'S PUBLISHING SERVICES


© J. D. Sainsbury 1988



**British Library Cataloguing in Publication Data**
Sainsbury, J. D. (John David), *1938–*
 The Hertfordshire Regiment: an illustrated
history.
 1. Great Britain. Army. Hertfordshire
Regiment to 1987
 I. Title
 355.3'7'094258

 ISBN 0–948555–16–5



Set in 10/11 Palatino
by Input Typesetting Ltd., London SW19 8DR
Printed and Bound in Great Britain by
Anchor Brendon Ltd., Tiptree, Essex.

# Preface

It is a rare privilege to be invited to write the history of a regiment of the British Army but a very considerable responsibility actually to do so. I have discharged this responsibility as well as I am able, in the knowledge that there will inevitably be those who feel the job should, in one respect or another, have been done differently. I firmly believe, however, that the point has been reached when all should agree that it is better that this book should appear now, rather than a 'perfect' history later, which I believe would turn out to be never. Accordingly, in honour of the Hertfordshire Regiment and their predecessors and successors, from Napoleonic times to the present day, I offer this history, all too conscious that it is not complete. Where opinions are expressed they are mine unless attributed otherwise and I alone am responsible for errors and omissions. I commend those who feel that there are, indeed, omissions to the sources for more detailed research outlined in Chapter Nine.

J. D. Sainsbury

Digswell, Welwyn,
Hertfordshire
*January 1988*

# Acknowledgements

Research leading to this history has gone on for nearly thirty years, during which I have made many friends among former and serving members of the Regiment and among those professionally responsible for its records in Government Departments, libraries and museums, as well as private collectors of 'militaria'. To all of them and to the following organisations I express my thanks:

Army Museums Ogilby Trust
Bank of England Libraries
Corporation of London – Guildhall Library
East Anglia Territorial, Auxiliary and Volunteer Reserve
    Association
Hertford Museum
Hertfordshire Army Cadet Force
Hertfordshire Library Service (especially Hertford Library,
    Watford Library and Welwyn Garden City Library)
Hitchin Museum
Imperial War Museum – Department of Printed Books
Inspector of Regimental Colours
Ministry of Defence – Army Historical Branch and Library
National Army Museum – Department of Records
Public Record Office
Regimental Headquarters The Royal Anglian Regiment

I must also record my particular thanks to Henry Gray and to the late Geoffrey Mussett for their remarkable drawings of Colours and badges and to Peter Davies, Peter Peacock and the late Fred Sellens for their skilled and enthusiastic help in photographing badges and paintings and copying old photographs. Permission to reproduce photographs has kindly been given by many copyright owners; acknowledgement appears beside each illustration. Every effort has been made to trace the owners of copyright but if I have inadvertently failed to do so my unreserved apologies are offered. Extracts from Crown Copyright publications and records appear by permission of the Controller of Her Majesty's Stationery Office.

Finally, I would like to thank those who have taken part in the preparation of the manuscript and in the assembly of the illustrations, or have otherwise given help and encouragement, especially Melanie Crick and Valerie Sherwood, Colin Albany, Terry Bell, Bill Carman, Gordon Davies, Alan Fleck, Peter Gray, Keith Hook, Alan Mollison, John Tamplin, Peter Walne, Peter Ward, Len Webb and Ray Westlake.

J.D.S.

# Contents

# Colour Plates

# Chapter 1

# *Historical Background to the Volunteer and Territorial Infantry*

The year 1794 is generally taken as the starting point of the volunteer forces which eventually grew into the Territorial Army. Although the principle of raising volunteers in time of emergency had long been recognised, only a very few units were legally constituted on a continuous basis before this time, and none of these was in Hertfordshire.

The rise of the mighty armies of Revolutionary France and the imminent threat of invasion led the Secretary of State for War to send a circular letter to Lords Lieutenant in March 1794, suggesting the desirability of opening subscription funds in their counties to support locally raised defence forces. It was proposed to raise these forces under four categories, namely: individual volunteers to augment Militia battalions; independent corps of volunteer infantry, especially in coastal districts; 'fencible' cavalry with terms of service approximately equivalent to the Militia; and other bodies of cavalry within particular counties or districts formed from the local 'Gentlemen and Yeomanry'. These measures were enacted in the Volunteer Act of April 1794 with the important proviso that the services of the volunteer troops should be accepted 'for the duration of the present war' only. The Act gave exemption from the Militia ballot to efficient members of the volunteer forces. Arms and accoutrements were to be supplied by Ordnance: arrangements for the supply of uniforms varied, some units receiving them from government sources, while others bought them out of the subscription fund. Regular training was carried out, some of it paid, and the volunteers were liable to be called out for permanent duty in the event of actual or impending invasion or in case of riot or civil commotion.

Further steps to secure the defence of the country were taken in 1797, when the government suggested that all parishes should form associations to organise their own local defence. Legislation was passed, as the Defence of the Realm Act of April 1798, permitting these associations to raise cavalry and infantry volunteers, provided that no expense fell on the government. In many cases, however, the government relented to the extent of supplying arms and accoutrements.

At the conclusion of the Peace of Amiens in March 1802 the volunteer forces were stood down but in a circular letter to Lords Lieutenant thanking the volunteers for their services, the Secretary of State for War pointed out that no treaty had been signed and asked that they should 'hold themselves in readiness for immediate service and be regularly trained and exercised . . .' As a result of this appeal many corps indicated their willingness to continue their services. Since the power to raise volunteer forces contained in the Acts of 1794 and 1798 had lapsed on the cessation of hostilities, a further Volunteer Act was passed almost [1] immediately to enable the government to accept the offers of the volunteer corps to continue their services during the peace and providing for the raising of new corps.

In May 1803 war was resumed. Volunteer corps in suspended animation resuscitated themselves and offered their services again. Many new corps were raised and most of those already in existence were reorganised and increased in strength on re-acceptance, their officers receiving new commissions. An effort was made to rationalise the organisation of the volunteer forces and companies were urged to join together into battalions for ease of administration and better tactical training. It was found necessary to revise existing legislation covering the volunteer forces and in June 1804 the Volunteer Consolidation Act was passed. This Act remained in force as the enabling legislation for the volunteer infantry until superseded by the Volunteer Act of 1863.

By 1806 the overall strength of the volunteer forces exceeded 370 000 – cavalry 32 000, infantry 329 000, artillery 10 000 – but as Napoleon's power began to dwindle, so did the threat of invasion and the need for such a large volunteer army. In an effort to reduce the number of infantry volunteers, but at the same time increase their efficiency and usefulness, the government raised the Local Militia in 1808 and encouraged the transfer of the volunteer infantry to the new force. Many corps, at least in part, accepted the new terms of service and transferred. Those that did not had all been disbanded by March 1813 and the country was without volunteer infantry. (In contrast, the Yeomanry Cavalry were kept in being, principally because of their value in aid of the Civil Power in the event of internal disorder.)

The threat of invasion from France had again grown to such an extent by the spring of 1859 that popular opinion forced the government once more to make provision for the Regular forces to be supported by volunteers. A circular letter to Lords Lieutenant of 12 May 1859 sanctioned the formation of volunteer rifle and artillery corps under the provisions of the 1804 Volunteer Act. The force was shortly afterwards extended to include engineer, mounted rifle and light horse volunteer corps. Later medical, supply and transport and other supporting units were authorised. The Volunteer Act of 1804 was not entirely satisfactory as the enabling legislation for the new force, and a new Volunteer Act was passed in July 1863 removing from the 1804 Act the authority for all volunteer troops except the Yeomanry Cavalry. The new Act brought up to date the administrative and disciplinary arrangements for volunteer forces, which could now be maintained on a permanent footing in peace time. Volunteers were liable to be called out in case of actual or apprehended invasion, whereas under the earlier Act they could not be called out until the invasion was seen to be impending from the 'appearance of the enemy in force upon the coast'. There was no specific provision in the new Act for the Volunteer Force to be used in the event of riot or civil commotion.

War Office Circulars dated 13 July 1859 and 24 March 1860 set out the organisation of the Force. The local unit was the corps, which could be as small as thirty men under a lieutenant but in large towns occasionally reached battalion strength. Normally corps consisted of one or two companies of infantry or equivalent strength in other arms. For ease of administration and for tactical training at higher levels infantry corps were grouped into 'administrative battalions' without infringing the self-governing nature of the corps in such matters as appointment of officers and N.C.O.s, dress (although the constituent corps of a battalion were encouraged to dress alike) and the holding of funds and property. In 1880 instructions were issued for infantry corps to be consolidated at battalion level.[1] In most cases the old administrative unit was redesignated a corps. The autonomy of the constituent local corps was considerably reduced and they were redesignated as lettered companies within their battalions. Alliances between administrative battalions of the Volunteer Force and the Regular battalions recruited in their areas were first set out in the sub-district brigade scheme of 1873.[2] These alliances continued when the regimental districts were established in 1881 and most rifle volunteer corps were eventually redesignated as Volunteer battalions of their parent Regular regiments. Battalions were first brigaded for training and administrative purposes in July 1888,[3] forming nineteen volunteer infantry brigades. In January 1902 the brigades were extensively reorganised to form in all forty-six brigades.

Volunteer battalions were invited to form companies to reinforce their allied Regular battalions during the South African War; those battalions whose companies served abroad for the necessary period were awarded the battle honour 'South Africa' with the appropriate dates.

Under Lord Haldane's scheme for the reorganisation of the reserve forces, the volunteer army was for the first time to be organised and equipped on the same lines as the Regular Army. Thus the Territorial Force, formed under the Territorial and Reserve Forces Act of 1907, was to consist of fourteen infantry divisions, including supporting troops, fourteen mounted brigades, and garrison and coast-defence units. The Act provided for the transfer of units of both the Imperial Yeomanry (as the Yeomanry Cavalry had by now become) and the Volunteer Force to the Territorial Force. There was accordingly no shortage of cavalry and infantry, but to make good the deficiencies in other arms large numbers of new units were formed, frequently by transfer of cadres from the Volunteer Force. (The original order of battle and the arrangements for the transfer of units and the provision of cadres are shown in detail in Army Order 70 of 1908.) It should be noted that the Volunteer Act, 1863 and its subsequent amendments were not repealed and served as the enabling legislation for the Volunteer Force raised during the First World War (see page 123).

The Territorial Force was for home defence and its officers and soldiers could not be required to serve outside the United Kingdom. It was possible, however, to accept a liability to go abroad on embodiment by volunteering for 'Imperial Service'. After mobilisation in August 1914 it was clear that the best use of Territorial units could only be made if they served abroad and efforts were made to encourage whole units to volunteer. In general they did so, though not all went to the Front at once, and '2nd-Line' units were formed from men who did not volunteer or were not of the required medical standard. These units were originally intended for home service only but many eventually served abroad. In 1915 '3rd-Line' training units were authorised, most of which were later absorbed into training centres and depots. The Territorial Force was demobilised in 1919. Units which had existed before the war were dispersed at their home stations and for a time existed only 'on paper', while those raised during the war were disbanded.

The Territorial Force did not remain inactive for long, for recruiting began again early in 1920. There was, however, an important change in the conditions of service, and recruits were only accepted on undertaking a liability to serve in any part of the world on embodiment. The order

of battle was substantially revised to provide a properly balanced force fit
for the new kind of warfare which had developed in the last few years.
The importance of horsed cavalry had greatly diminished, and out of over
fifty regiments of Yeomanry only seventeen retained their horses. The
remainder were converted to units of the Royal Tank Corps, Royal Artillery
or Royal Signals while keeping their Yeomanry titles and traditions. The
first of many Territorial anti-aircraft units of the Royal Artillery and Royal
Engineers were also formed. In October 1921, with the coming into force
of the Territorial Army and Militia Act, 1921, the Territorial Force was
renamed the 'Territorial Army' and became the only authorised auxiliary
military force in the United Kingdom apart from the Militia (formerly
Special Reserve), which had not been re-formed after the war. The legislation permitting other volunteer forces was revoked. (Hence the need for
new legislation to cover the raising of the Home Guard in 1940 and again
in 1952 – see pages 128 and 132) The revised order of battle for the
Territorial Army and the arrangements for conversion to other arms, both
of which took some time to agree, were published with Army Order 482
of 1922. An amended version was published with Army Order 390 of 1927.
Thereafter details of conversions, disbandments and the formation of new
units can be traced individually in Army Orders or, from mid-1939 until
some time after mobilisation, in Army Council Instructions.

The worsening international situation in the late 1930s led first to a big
increase in the number of Territorial anti-aircraft units. As the threat of
war grew it was decided in March 1939 to bring the whole of the Territorial
Army up to war establishment and then to double the number of field
force units. The doubling was achieved by forming 'duplicate' units, often
incorrectly referred to as '2nd-Line' units although there was no similarity
between them and the 2nd-Line units of 1914: terms of service were
identical throughout the Territorial Army and no units were specifically
designated 'Reserve' or 'Training'. By the outbreak of war in September
1939 the duplication had been substantially completed. On mobilisation
units were brought up to strength with reservists, as far as possible from
their own counties, but thereafter Territorial units were, for the purpose
of reinforcement, treated exactly as Regular units and gradually became
'diluted' with men from other counties. This was in marked contrast to
the system in the first few years of the First World War when a volunteer
could be reasonably certain of serving with his county regiment. Territorial
units which became surplus to requirements during the war or had to be
broken up to provide reinforcements were not disbanded put placed in
'suspended animation' so that they could be re-formed after the war.
Similarly, units were placed in 'suspended animation' on demobilisation
in 1946.

The Territorial Army was re-formed in 1947. There was a further extensive revision of the order of battle but generally speaking all pre-war
'original' units were included, even if after a change of arm. There were
more reorganisations as circumstances changed, particularly with the
disbandment of Anti-Aircraft Command in 1955 and of the Coast Artillery
in 1956. Where possible units were amalgamated rather than disbanded.
The Territorial Army was made responsible for the part-time training of
national servicemen, who were posted to local units for three years after
their full-time service. By the late 1950s, though still liable for part-time
service, national servicemen were no longer required to attend for training,
and an all-volunteer Territorial Army gradually re-emerged. A further
reorganisation was deemed necessary in 1960, and was justified in a White

Paper published in November.[4] The proposed amalgamations were to be completed by 1 May 1961.

By February 1965 a root-and-branch reform of the Army's voluntary reserves – the Territorial Army and the Army Emergency Reserve – was being widely forecast. At the end of July the Government made clear their intentions in a statement in the House of Commons. They proposed that the future role of the voluntary reserves would be threefold – to provide individuals and a few units liable to call-out at any time to reinforce the Regular Army, to reinforce and support the Regular Army in limited war, and to provide reinforcements for N.A.T.O. in accordance with United Kingdom commitments. The establishment of the new force would only be some 50 000. There would be very few 'teeth arms' units, including only thirteen infantry battalions – one for each Regular infantry brigade or large regiment. More than half of the force would comprise logistic units. Territorial formations (brigades and divisions), which for some years had had no mobilisation role as such, would be abolished and units would be assigned directly to the Regular formation with which they would fight after mobilisation. Opposition to the plan began almost at once and continued over a period of nearly two years, achieving a significant modification, for when the outline plan for the 'Army Volunteer Reserve', as the new force was to be called, was published as a White Paper[5] in December 1965 the Government admitted that they were 'continuing their examination of how best to secure appropriate provision for home defence and what contribution military units might best make towards this'. In February 1966 it was announced that an additional force of 28 000 would be established, organised in 'lightly armed units of infantry type'. Their primary role would be 'to assist the police in maintaining law and order in the event of a nuclear threat and to act generally in support of the civil authorities'. It was further recognised that such units would provide a useful basis for expansion should the need arise. During April and May 1966 further details of the plans for the new reserve, now to be called the 'Territorial and Army Volunteer Reserve', were announced, including the order of battle of the Home Defence element, which was to comprise eighty-seven infantry units and a small number of signal troops. The necessary legislation was passed as the Reserve Forces Act, 1966, the effect of which, together with Orders and Royal Warrants issued early in 1967, was to form the Territorial and Army Volunteer Reserve on 1 April 1967 from the Territorial Army and the Army Emergency Reserve.

The Territorial and Army Volunteer Reserve was initially raised in four categories with differing liabilities for training and call-out:

*Categories I, IIA* and *IIB*, collectively known as 'Volunteers', had a substantial training commitment and undertook to serve outside the United Kingdom on embodiment. They were equipped to a scale approximating to that of equivalent units of the Regular Army.

*Category III*, known as 'Territorials', had a reduced training commitment and could be called out only for service in the United Kingdom. All Category III units except signal troops were equipped to a light scale of infantry equipment, regardless of their designated arm.

*Category IV* consisted of a small number of specialist units, pools of individual reinforcements (largely officers), authorised bands and units of the Officers Training Corps. Their terms of service were broadly similar to Categories I and II.

The transition to the Territorial and Army Volunteer Reserve involved the reduction in status and strength of many Territorial Army units and some changes of arm. Comparatively few units were disbanded. This course was amply justified by the opportunity which it gave to new units to carry on the history and traditions of their predecessors once re-equipped and reorganised in their new role. The full list of original Territorial and Army Volunteer Reserve units and their succession from Territorial Army or Army Emergency Reserve units is given in Army Orders 2 and 5 of 1967. The separateness of the Territorials was assured by the Territorial Force for Home Service Warrant, 1967, published as Army Order 3 of 1967. For the first time since 1908 the volunteer army, with the exception of the parachute battalions, was no longer to be organised in its own formations. The headquarters of the old Territorial brigades and divisions were disbanded and units were fitted into the Regular Army's command structure, both in the British Army of the Rhine, to which most of Categories IIA and IIB were assigned, and at home.

In January 1968 it was announced that Category III of the Territorial and Army Volunteer Reserve was to be disbanded, together with the greater part of the Civil Defence services. Although the active strength of Civil Defence Corps and Auxiliary Fire Service volunteers was dispersed soon afterwards, no action was taken to disband military units, and it was later announced that Category III would be permitted to continue recruiting and training pending a further review of the Reserve Forces, provided that no expense fell to public funds. Most units did continue on these terms and many went to camp in the summer of 1968 on a self-supporting basis. The result of the futher review was disclosed late in November 1968. The four categories of the Territorial and Army Volunteer Reserve were to be amalgamated and all units become liable to serve abroad on mobilisation, though training commitments would still differ. Former Category I and II units comprised 'Group A' of the reorganised force, while former Category IV units were included in Group B. (A third group – Group C – was later raised – see below.)

The changeover to the new organisation under a new Order published as Army Order 26 of 1969 was effective on 1 April 1969 and all Category III units were disbanded on 31 March 1969. The titles of ninety Category III units were retained by the raising in Group A of representative cadres of eight officers and soldiers, each 'sponsored' by, and to train as part of, a Group A unit, not necessarily infantry. The function of the cadres was to provide 'nuclei around which units could be formed when minor changes are made in the T. & A.V.R. order of battle'.

Surprisingly, perhaps, no action was taken to ensure that the cadres were the legal successors to the Category III units whose titles they perpetuated. However, it was widely publicised that they would hold the property, and where appropriate the Colours, of these units and they were without doubt their *de facto* successors. Many of the former Category IIA units were authorised to increase their strength to 140 per cent of normal establishment, and in some cases the extra strength was used to raise new sub-units. A revised schedule of the units and independent sub-units of the reorganised Territorial and Army Volunteer Reserve was published with Army Order 26 of 1969. Regrettably this does not show the cadres individually but a comprehensive list did appear in *Soldier*.[6] In February 1970 approval, back-dated to December 1969, was given for nine rifle companies (which had existed for some months in 'shadow' form within the overall increase in unit ceilings mentioned earlier) to be officially constituted as additional sub-units of their battalions.

A major expansion of the infantry component of the Territorial and Army Volunteer Reserve was announced in outline in the autumn of 1970 and in detail in January 1971. An additional twenty battalions would be formed. Fifteen of these (twelve designated as infantry and three as Yeomanry but organised and equipped as infantry) were to be given a 'General Reserve', role, that is they were not, as were all existing Volunteer infantry battalions, committed to the reinforcement of the British forces on the continent on mobilisation but would train and expect to be mobilised for the defence of the United Kingdom base. Most of the cadres of former Category III units were expanded to provide companies within the twenty new battalions, which began to form in April 1971. Initially the scale of equipment of the General Reserve battalions was well below that of N.A.T.O. battalions but the gap has in general been made good in the years since formation. Headquarter companies were not authorised for General Reserve battalions until January 1981, though some battalions had been maintaining them on a 'shadow' basis in anticipation of the authority. (The number of rifle companies in a battalion varies between three and five.)

In September 1979 the title 'Territorial and Army Volunteer Reserve', which had been in dispute in many quarters since its introduction in 1967, was altered to 'Territorial Army' by Defence Council Instruction.[7] The alteration required confirmation by legislation, which surprisingly was not included in the Reserve Forces Act, 1980. This Act, which refers throughout to 'Territorial Army', consolidates earlier legislation relating to the Reserve Forces (including the Reserves of the Royal Navy, Royal Marines and the Royal Air Force) and replaces the Reserve Forces Act, 1966 as the enabling legislation for all Land Forces reserves except the Home Guard (see page 132). The change of title was finally confirmed by the Reserve Forces Act, 1982. Despite the change, units retained the designation 'Volunteer', which is incorporated in the titles of infantry battalions as either, for example '5th (Volunteer) Battalion The Royal Anglian Regiment' or as '1st Battalion The Yorkshire Volunteers'.

The June 1981 Defence Review foreshadowed a further expansion of the Territorial Army to take place between 1982 and 1989. This phased 'enhancement', as the process became known, would raise the recruiting ceiling from 70 000 to 86 000 by the addition of individual posts to unit establishments, by the raising of sub-units within existing units and by the formation of entire new units. The opportunity of reorganising existing units by re-allocating sub-units on a more sensible geographical basis was also taken. As part of Phase 1 of the enhancements, scheduled for completion during 1986, reconnaissance platoons were added to fifteen N.A.T.O. infantry battalions and three additional companies were formed, also in N.A.T.O. battalions. Phase 2, starting in 1986 and due for completion in 1989, includes the formation of six new infantry battalions, all with the General Reserve role. Much of the geographical rationalisation, though officially included in Phase 2, was carried out, or at least begun, before 1986.

The enhancement programme for N.A.T.O. and General Reserve units was paralleled by the development of a new organisation to provide manpower specifically for static guard tasks in the United Kingdom, also outlined in the 1981 Defence Review. Provision for the raising of a 'Home Service Force' stemming from the defunct 'Territorial Force for Home Service' was contained in the Reserve Forces Act, 1980, which stipulated that the Home Service Force was to be part of the Territorial Army, though engaged for service within the United Kingdom only. Terms of service were sufficiently different from those of the existing Groups A and B of the Territorial Army for a new group – Group C – to be introduced; at present Group C comprises only the Home Service Force. No additional authority similar to the Territorial Force for Home Service Warrant, 1967, was judged necessary and the executive authority for the raising of the force was promulgated by Ministry of Defence Letter and amendments to *Regulations for the Territorial Army*. The similarity between the Home Service Force and the earlier National Reserve and National Defence Companies, raised in association with the Territorial Force and Territorial Army, respectively, is such that it is included with these predecessors in Chapter Seven.

NOTES

1. Auxiliary and Reserve Forces Circulars dated 3 February and 17 April 1880

2. Auxiliary and Reserve Forces Circular dated 8 April 1873

3. A.O. 314/1888

4. Cmnd. 1216

5. Cmnd. 2855

6. Volume 26, No. 10, October 1970

7. D.C.I. (Army) J 284/1979

# Chapter 2

# *The Armed Associations and Volunteer Infantry in Hertfordshire 1798–1809*

Although the measures taken in 1794 to provide additional volunteer troops for home defence permitted the raising of volunteer infantry units, none were in fact raised in Hertfordshire. The county waited until the passing of the Defence of the Realm Act in 1798 (see page 1) and then participated actively in the formation of infantry armed associations for local defence. Ten such associations were formed, as shown in detail in Table 2.1. An association may also have been formed at Cottered but if it did ever stand as a body it was only for a short time. Each association was commanded by a captain, assisted by a lieutenant and an ensign (second lieutenant), indicating that their establishments, which may not all have been the same, would have been between 80 and 120.

Undoubtedly the high spot in the history of the early Hertfordshire associations was the Review by King George III in Hatfield Park on 13 June 1800. The occasion was fully described by Lord Salisbury in his privately published *Narrative* (see Bibliography) and forms the subject of an oil painting by Richard Livesay which hangs in Hatfield House. (Livesay also did water colours of the Review and subsequently published a coloured engraving.) A table showing the parade states of the

[9]

TABLE 2.1    *Volunteer Infantry (Armed Associations) in Hertfordshire 1798–1802*[1]

| | |
|---|---|
| *Stanstead Abbots and Hunsdon*<br>Raised 17 May 1798; disbanded March 1802 | Blue |
| *Bishop's Stortford*<br>Raised 23 May 1798; stood down March 1802; re-formed August 1803 | Blue, facings red |
| *Cheshunt*<br>Raised 23 May 1798; stood down March 1802; amalgamated with Wormley Volunteer Infantry on re-formation August 1803 | Blue |
| *Hatfield*<br>Raised 23 May 1798; stood down March 1802; re-formed as part of 1st Regiment Hertfordshire Volunteer Infantry August 1803 | Blue |
| *Wormley*<br>Raised 23 May 1798; stood down March 1802; amalgamated with Cheshunt Volunteer Infantry on re-formation August 1803 | Blue |
| *St. Albans*[2]<br>Raised 24 May 1798; stood down March 1802; re-formed September 1803 | Red, facings blue |
| *Ware*<br>Raised 24 May 1798; stood down March 1802; re-formed September 1803 | Blue |
| *Hertford*<br>Raised 28 May 1798; stood down March 1802; re-formed September 1803 | Blue |
| *Royston*<br>Raised 12 June 1798; stood down March 1802; re-formed September 1803 | Blue |
| *Hitchin (Loyal)*<br>Raised 13 July 1798; stood down March 1802; re-formed August 1803 | Blue, facings red |

[1] The dates of formation shown are those of the Government's acceptance of the associations' offers of service, which were used for the captains' commissions and in assessing the precedence of units. Many, if not all, of the associations were formed several months earlier. It is, for instance, known that the Hitchin Association was formed by resolution of 28 April 1798 and was sixty strong by mid-May.

[2] The St. Albans Association is also shown as cavalry in the *Army List* but the cavalry element of this association, if it ever existed, was very short-lived.

associations, which was included in the *Narrative*, is reproduced at Figure 2.2. Livesay required members of the various associations to come to his studio in uniform so that he could ensure correct detail in the painting. The infantry associations are shown marching past the King (see Figure 2.3) and hence are in the middle distance. Nevertheless the painting provides a remarkable contemporary record of the uniforms worn by the associations between their formation and the Peace of Amiens. The St. Albans Association was the only one with red coats – all the others wore blue – and hence can be precisely identified. Since the order of the march past is recorded, some other associations can also be recognised, but not all are visible.

In May 1800 Charles Bridgeman, organist of All Saints' Church, Hertford, and himself a member of the Hertford Association, wrote and published in one volume slow and quick marches for all ten associations, some scored for full band, some for fife only. Examples of this music

# FIELD RETURN of the Troops reviewed by HIS MAJESTY, in Hatfield Park, Friday, 13 June, 1800.

| | Captains. | Lieut. | Ensigns. | Surgeon. | Chaplain. | Quarter-Masters. | Adjutant. | Sergeant Majors. | Sergeants. | Pioneer. | Drums and Fifes. | Rank and File. | Total. |
|---|---|---|---|---|---|---|---|---|---|---|---|---|---|
| HUNSDON | 1 | ... | 1 | ... | ... | ... | ... | ... | 2 | ... | ... | 35 | 39 |
| CHESHUNT | 1 | 1 | 1 | ... | ... | ... | ... | ... | 3 | ... | 2 | 40 | 48 |
| WORMLEY | 1 | ... | ... | ... | ... | ... | ... | ... | 1 | ... | 2 | 22 | 26 |
| HATFIELD | 1 | 2 | 1 | ... | ... | ... | ... | 1 | 4 | ... | 4 | 64 | 77 |
| BISHOP'S STORTFORD | 1 | 1 | 1 | ... | ... | ... | ... | ... | 2 | ... | 1 | 50 | 56 |
| ST. ALBAN'S | 1 | 2 | ... | 1 | 1 | ... | ... | 1 | 4 | ... | 5 | 59 | 74 |
| WARE | 1 | 1 | 1 | ... | ... | ... | ... | ... | 4 | 1 | 4 | 64 | 76 |
| HARTFORD | 1 | 1 | 1 | ... | ... | ... | ... | ... | 7 | ... | 4 | 89 | 103 |
| ROYSTON | 1 | 1 | 1 | ... | ... | 1 | 1 | ... | 3 | ... | 4 | 58 | 72 |
| HITCHIN | 1 | 2 | 1 | ... | ... | .. | ... | ... | 5 | ... | 3 | 60 | 71 |
| Infantry | 10 | 11 | 8 | 1 | 1 | 1 | 1 | 2 | 36 | 1 | 29 | 541 | 643 |
| | | | Cornets. | | | | | | | | Trumpets | | |
| Honorable Captain LAMB | 1 | 1 | 1 | ... | ... | ... | ... | ... | 1 | ... | 1 | 64 | 69 |
| Captain HALE | 1 | 1 | 1 | ... | ... | 1 | ... | ... | 1 | ... | 1 | 54 | 60 |
| Captain CALVERT | 1 | 1 | 1 | ... | ... | ... | ... | ... | 1 | ... | 1 | 64 | 69 |
| Honorable Captain VILLIERS | 1 | 1 | ... | ... | ... | ... | ... | ... | 1 | ... | 1 | 41 | 45 |
| Captain HANKIN | 1 | 1 | 1 | ... | ... | ... | ... | ... | ... | ... | ... | 38 | 41 |
| Captain Sir GEORGE PRESCOT, Bart. | 1 | 1 | ... | ... | ... | ... | ... | ... | 1 | ... | 1 | 56 | 60 |
| Captain Sir ABRAHAM HUME, Bart. | 1 | ... | 1 | ... | ... | ... | ... | ... | 1 | ... | ... | 31 | 34 |
| Captain Sir JOHN SEBRIGHT, Bart. | 1 | 1 | ... | ... | ... | ... | ... | ... | ... | ... | ... | 42 | 45 |
| Cavalry | 8 | 7 | 6 | ... | ... | 1 | ... | ... | 6 | ... | 5 | 390 | 433 |
| Total | 18 | 18 | 14 | 1 | 1 | 2 | 1 | 2 | 42 | 1 | 34 | 931 | 1065 |

Figure 2.2 *The Royal Review in Hatfield Park, June 1800 – Parade state (described as 'Field Return') of the Volunteers taking part in the Review. The numbers of infantry on parade may be compared with the establishments of the various associations shown in Table 2.1*

(Hertfordshire County Record Office)

Figure 2.3 *Detail from the oil painting by Richard Livesay showing the Volunteer Associations marching past. The St. Albans Association, in red coats, are at far left.*

(© The Most Hon. The Marquess of Salisbury)

Figure 2.4 *Hertfordshire Volunteer Associations – A page from Charles Bridgeman's marches for the Hertfordshire Volunteers, published in 1800 and believed to have been played at the Royal Review in Hatfield Park (see Figures 2.1–2.3). Bridgeman was organist at All Saints' Church, Hertford, and a member of the Hertford Volunteers.*

(British Library)

survive and a page is reproduced at Figure 2.4. It is generally assumed that Bridgeman's marches were used at the Royal Review.

Many of the Hertfordshire associations offered to continue their services during the Peace of Amiens but no record of official acceptance of these offers has yet been traced. It may be assumed that, if not actually disbanded, they all ceased training and went into what would now be called 'suspended animation'.

When the volunteer infantry was once again required in 1803 the opportunity was taken to increase considerably the county's overall establishment – to about 2500, as against less than 700 in 1798 – and several units consisting of more than one company were raised.

The new 'order of battle' is shown in detail in Table 2.2. There was considerable delay in promulgating the acceptance of offers of service, with the result that the precedence of corps, and of officers' commissions, date between 12 August and 13 September 1803. Many of the corps had in fact offered their services and assembled for training within days of the resumption of hostilities in May.

Considerable attention was paid to the organisation of the county's volunteers on mobilisation. As early as December 1803 the Lord Lieutenant wrote to the officers commanding all local units pointing out 'the propriety and real advantage of forming the independent companies of volunteers into regiments and brigades' but, in deference to the strong local sensibilities that were a feature of the volunteers (and are of their successors, even to the present day), promising that 'your men will continue to be drilled where they usually meet and you will have no additional trouble but that when called out you will form battalions and the different battalions a brigade'. The proposed battalions were not given designations but were to be formed as shown in Table 2.3. (The Kimpton Rifles were omitted from the scheme, presumably in order to allow them to operate in a scouting role in keeping with their designation.)

It was clearly desirable that the troops forming the brigade should be dressed alike. Regulations already required all volunteer infantry except

TABLE 2.2   *Volunteer Infantry in Hertfordshire 1803–1809*

| | |
|---|---|
| *Bishop's Stortford Volunteer Infantry* | Red, facings black; |
| Re-formed from earlier volunteer association 12 August 1803 with an establishment of 200 in three companies; disbanded 17 March 1809 | lace gold |
| *Hitchin Volunteer Infantry* | Red, facings yellow |
| Re-formed from earlier volunteer assocation 12 August 1803 with an establishment of 300 in three companies; fourth company raised October 1804; companies numbered 1st to 4th by seniority of their captains; detachments at Hexton, Pirton, St. Ippollitts and Ickleford; disbanded 15 March 1809; partially absorbed into the Midland Regiment of Hertfordshire Local Militia | |
| *Loyal Hemel Hempstead Volunteer Infantry* | Red, facings yellow; |
| Raised 12 August 1803 with an establishment of 100 in one company; disbanded 1808; partially absorbed into the Western Regiment of Hertfordshire Local Militia | lace silver |
| *Hertfordshire Rifles* | Green, facings black; |
| Raised 12 August 1803 at Kimpton with an establishment of 120 in two companies; disbanded 11 March 1809; partially absorbed into the Midland Regiment of Hertfordshire Local Militia | lace black |

(Continued overleaf)

Table 2.2 (*Continued*)

| | |
|---|---|
| *1st Regiment Hertfordshire Volunteer Infantry*<br>Raised 20 August 1803 with an establishment of 500 in six companies – Hatfield, North Mimms, Brocket Hall, Northaw, Shenley and Ridge, and Wheathampstead and Welwyn; seventh company formed April 1804 by separation of Welwyn and Wheathampstead; disbanded 15 August 1808; partially absorbed into the Midland Regiment of Hertfordshire Local Militia | Red, facings yellow; no lace |
| *Cheshunt and Wormley Volunteer Infantry*<br>Re-formed from earlier volunteer associations 20 August 1803 with an establishment of 100 in one company; incorporated in the South Hertfordshire Legion; disbanded March 1809 | Red, facings black; lace gold |
| *Hertford Volunteer Infantry*<br>Re-formed from earlier volunteer association 5 September 1803 with an establishment of 160 in two companies; reduced to one company by 1807; disbanded 1809 | Red, facings yellow; no lace |
| *Standon Volunteer Infantry*<br>Raised 5 September 1803 with an establishment of 90 in one company; disbanded March 1809; partially absorbed into the Eastern Regiment of Hertfordshire Local Militia | |
| *St. Albans Volunteer Infantry*<br>Re-formed from earlier volunteer association 13 September 1803 with an establishment of 240 in three companies – 1st (St. Stephens) Company, 2nd (Redbourn and St. Michaels) Company, 3rd (Abbey) Company; disbanded 11 March 1809; partially absorbed into the Western Regiment of Hertfordshire Local Militia | Red, facings yellow; lace gold |
| *Bayford and Essendon Volunteer Infantry*<br>Raised 13 September 1803 with an establishment of 80 in one company; disbanded 19 May 1806 | Red, facings yellow; no lace |
| *Royston and Barkway Volunteer Infantry*<br>Re-formed from earlier volunteer association 13 September 1803 with an establishment of 150 in two companies; disbanded 24 March 1809 | Red, facings blue; lace gold |
| *East and Chipping Barnet Volunteer Infantry*<br>Raised 13 September 1803 with an establishment of 120 in one company; disbanded 20 June 1807 | Red, facings blue; lace gold |
| *Ware Volunteer Infantry*<br>Re-formed from earlier volunteer association 13 September 1803 with an establishment of 80 in one company; absorbed into 2nd Regiment Hertfordshire Volunteer Infantry 12 August 1805 | |
| *Watford Volunteer Infantry*<br>Raised 13 September 1803 with an establishment of 130 in two companies (the second company appears never to have been formed); disbanded March 1809; partially absorbed into the Western Regiment of Hertfordshire Local Militia | Red, facings yellow; lace gold |
| *2nd Regiment Hertfordshire Volunteer Infantry*<br>Raised 5 March 1805 in the Hoddesdon and Stanstead district with an establishment of 180 in three companies; fourth company added shortly; absorbed Ware Volunteer Infantry and establishment increased to five companies 12 August 1805; companies designated Grenadier Company, Light Company, 1st, 2nd and 3rd Battalion Companies; disbanded 11 March 1809; partially absorbed into the Eastern Regiment of Hertfordshire Local Militia. | Red, facings yellow; lace gold |

Figure 2.5 (Left)  *St. Albans Volunteer Infantry – Officer's engraved gilt crossbelt plate, c. 1805.*
*(Actual size 63 mm. × 80 mm.)*                                         (Private collection)
(Right)  *Standon Volunteer Infantry – Officer's engraved gilt crossbelt plate, c. 1805. (Actual*
*size 61 mm. × 84 mm.)*                                              (Hertford Museum)

those designated rifles to wear red, in common with Regular and Militia infantry, and the Lord Lieutenant met with considerable success in persuading Hertfordshire units to adopt 'yellow' facings (probably, in fact, the sandy yellow or 'buff' of the Hertfordshire Militia), as can be seen in Table 2.2. A primitive initial deployment plan was drawn up and published, probably at the turn of the year 1805, in the form of the map reproduced at Figure 2.6. Under the plan some 670 men who assembled in the north and west of the county were to move southwards and east-wards to designated stations so that the infantry would be located south and east of a line through Barkway, Stevenage, Kimpton and St. Albans.

It can be seen from Figure 2.6 and from Table 2.2 that a substantial

TABLE 2.3   *The Lord Lieutenant's Scheme for Forming Battalions on Call-Out,*
*December 1803*

| Corps | Strength | Corps | Strength | Corps | Strength |
|---|---|---|---|---|---|
| Bayford | 80 | St. Albans | 240 | Hitchin | 300 |
| Ware | 90 | Watford | 120 | Hatfield | 500 |
| Standon | 90 | Hemel Hempstead | 100 | | |
| Hertford | 160 | Barnet | 120 | | |
| Bishop's Stortford | 240 | Royston | 150 | | |
| Wormley | 100 | | | | |
| *Total* | 760 | *Total* | 730 | *Total* | 800 |

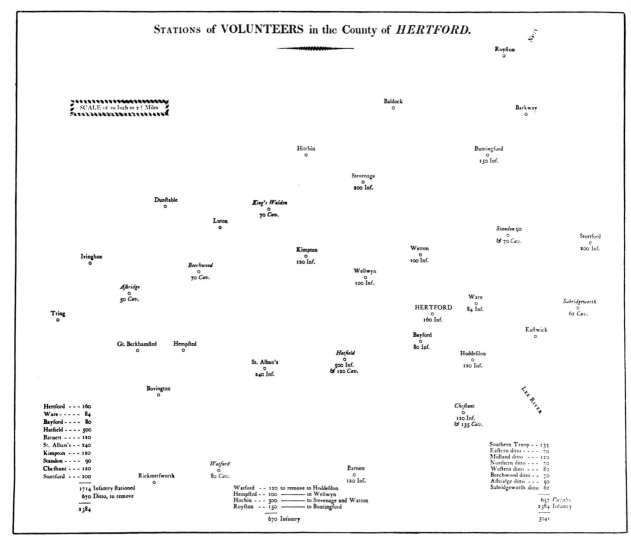

STATIONS of **VOLUNTEERS** in the County of *HERTFORD*.

Figure 2.6  *Hertfordshire Volunteer Associations – Map showing the 'Stations of Volunteers' on call-out, c. 1805. A primitive deployment plan provided for four infantry associations to 'remove' so that they were better placed to meet any enemy advance from the south-east.*
(Hertfordshire County Record Office)

additional unit, eventually known as the 2nd Regiment of Hertfordshire Volunteer Infantry was raised early in 1805. The peak of volunteer strength and effort in the county, as elsewhere, is likely to have been reached in 1806–07, coinciding with Willson's famous nationwide survey and the publication of his 'Chart', which shows a total volunteer infantry strength of just over three thousand in Hertfordshire, organised in fourteen units.

Deployment plans were supplemented by the earmarking in peacetime of wagons and carts for use in an emergency, both as transport and to form road blocks and obstacles to the progress of the invader. Inspectors of volunteers were appointed and corps were regularly inspected and exercised, the increased training commitment being met by an increase in the allocation of paid training days, up to a maximum of twenty-four days

Figure 2.7  *Hertfordshire Volunteer Associations – Crossbelt plate of the 2nd Regiment of Hertfordshire Volunteer Infantry (see Table 2.2) embodying the 'hart lodged' also used by the Hoddesdon and Stanstead Volunteer Association (see Figure 2.11) and providing evidence of the earliest use of this badge by Hertfordshire's Volunteer Infantry.*
(Drawing by Henry Gray from the original in the Reynolds Manuscripts, Victoria and Albert Museum)

per man per year. BUSBY quotes the 1806 Volunteer Returns as recording that the Kimpton, Hitchin and Bishop's Stortford Volunteers were passed by the Inspector as 'fit to act with troops of the Line', while the rest were 'advancing in discipline' except for Barnet and Standon, who were 'deficient in discipline' – comments that would bear comparison with those made at present-day 'Annual Review of Unit' and 'Fitness for Role' inspections!

Many, if not all, of the corps contrived to be presented with Colours. There do not appear to have been regulations about the carrying of Colours by the early volunteer infantry, as there were from 1860 onwards (see page 48) but Hertfordshire corps seem to have conformed to the conventions of the time and carried pairs of Colours (King's and Regimental) presented, if not actually provided, by local ladies of standing. Accounts of several of the presentation parades survive and the last pair of Colours to be presented – to the Hoddesdon and Stanstead Volunteers (later the 2nd Regiment of Hertfordshire Volunteer Infantry) – are preserved in Hertford Castle, together with the King's Colour of the Hertford Volunteers. As far as can be established, all the Colours were painted on silk (a normal practice at the time) rather than embroidered. Reconstructions of the King's and the Regimental Colours of the Hoddesdon and Stanstead Volunteers and the King's Colour of the Hertford Volunteers already referred to and the Regimental Colour of the Royston and Barkway Volunteers, which can be discerned from a photograph in Royston Museum, are reproduced as Figures 2.8, 2.9, 2.10 and 2.11.

Pressure on the volunteers to transfer to the newly formed Local Militia began late in 1808. Early the following year it must have become clear that the only way to remain in uniform was to transfer, for by the end of March 1809 all Hertfordshire units had disbanded, with substantial numbers accepting the changed terms of service and re-mustering with one of the three Hertfordshire battalions of the Local Militia. The thread of the Volunteers, as opposed to the Militia, in Hertfordshire was broken for some fifty years until volunteers were once again raised, under the same legislation that had covered those just described, in 1859-60.

Figure 2.8   *Hertfordshire Volunteer Associations – King's Colour of the Hertford Volunteers,*
*painted on silk, c. 1803, now in the care of Hertford Town Council. (Actual size 1.95 m. × 1.80 m.)*
(Drawing by Henry Gray)

Figure 2.9   *Hertfordshire Volunteer Associations – Regimental Colour of the Royston and Barkway Volunteers, painted on silk,* c. *1803. (Actual size 1.95 m. × 1.80 m.)*

(Drawing by Geoffrey Mussett)

Figure 2.10   *Hertfordshire Volunteer Associations – King's Colour of the Hoddesdon and Stanstead Volunteers, painted on silk, c. 1805, now in the care of Hertford Town Council. (Actual size 1.95 m. × 1.80 m.)*
(Drawing by Henry Gray)

Figure 2.11   *Hertfordshire Volunteer Associations – Regimental Colour of the Hoddesdon and Stanstead Volunteers, painted on buff silk, c. 1805, now in the care of Hertford Town Council. (Actual size 1.95 m. × 1.80 m.)*                              (Drawing by Geoffrey Mussett)

# Chapter 3

# *The Rifle Volunteers in Hertfordshire 1859–1908*

## 3.1  Hertfordshire Rifle Volunteers 1859–1887

The first corps of Rifle Volunteers to be formed in Hertfordshire was raised at Hertford following a meeting held there on 25 October 1859, at which members of the Hertford Rifle Club agreed to offer their services to Her Majesty. Acceptance of the corps – to be designated 1st Hertfordshire Rifle Volunteers and with an establishment of one company – was signified on 22 November 1859. By September 1860 twelve corps had been raised, some with 'sub-divisions' or drill stations in outlying towns or villages. In October 1860 the establishment of the 1st Hertfordshire Corps was increased to two companies. (The second company, which was described in the early years of its existence as 'consisting largely of artizans', held drill parades in the evenings, while the first company was composed of those who could attend afternoon parades without detriment to their businesses or careers.) Two administrative battalions were formed in October 1860 – the 1st Administrative Battalion incorporating six corps in the western half of the county and the 2nd Administrative Battalion with six corps in the eastern half. The 22nd Essex Rifle Volunteers at Waltham Abbey joined the 2nd Administrative Battalion in 1863. A 13th Corps was raised in 1864, only to be disbanded four years later. The 8th, 11th and 12th Corps were also disbanded or amalgamated with neighbouring corps between 1866 and 1870. The last numbered corps to be raised – the two-company 14th – proved longer lasting. Full details of the battalions and their constituent corps are given in Table 3.1. (It should be noted that the corps raised at Barnet in October 1859 was designated 12th Middlesex and that the Barnet Volunteers retained their association with Middlesex throughout, as described in Appendix 2.) Both administrative battalions were linked to the 33rd Sub-District Brigade Depot at Bedford in April 1873 – the start of the link between the Volunteer infantry of Hertfordshire and the Regular infantry regiment recruiting in Bedfordshire and Hertfordshire which persists today.

The numbered corps within the two administrative battalions were consolidated in 1880, when each battalion became a corps. At the same time, in accordance with instructions that consolidated corps should take the number of the most senior of their original constituent corps, the seniority of the two battalions, which had been numbered according to date of formation, was reversed, the 2nd Administrative Battalion becoming the 1st Hertfordshire Rifle Volunteer Corps and the 1st Administrative Battalion the 2nd. Within the new corps the companies lost their original numbers and were given the conventional lettered designations according to their former precedence, as shown in Table 3.2.

Although all the original numbered corps adopted a grey uniform (as did the majority of corps throughout the country) and there was thus a

TABLE 3.1 *Hertfordshire Rifle Volunteers 1860–1880*

| *1st Administrative Battalion*<br>Formed 16 October 1860<br>Headquarters: Little Gaddesden<br>Uniform: Grey, facings green | *2nd Administrative Battalion*<br>Formed 24 October 1860<br>Headquarters: Hertford<br>Uniform: Grey, facings scarlet |
|---|---|
| 2nd Hertfordshire Rifle Volunteers<br>(Watford)<br>Raised 5 January 1860 (C) | 1st Hertfordshire Rifle Volunteers<br>(Hertford)<br>1st Company raised 22 November 1859 (E)<br>2nd Company raised 26 October 1860 (C) |
| 3rd Hertfordshire Rifle Volunteers<br>(St. Albans)<br>Raised 5 March 1860 (E) | 6th Hertfordshire Rifle Volunteers<br>(Bishop's Stortford)<br>Raised 20 March 1860 (E) |
| 4th Hertfordshire Rifle Volunteers<br>(Ashridge)<br>Raised 1 March 1860 (C) | 9th Hertfordshire Rifle Volunteers<br>(Ware)<br>Raised 13 June 1860 (E) |
| 5th Hertfordshire Rifle Volunteers<br>(Hemel Hempstead)<br>Raised 10 March 1860 (C) | 10th Hertfordshire Rifle Volunteers<br>(Royston and Baldock)<br>Raised 25 June 1860 (C) |
| 7th Hertfordshire Rifle Volunteers<br>(Berkhamsted)<br>Raised 13 March 1860 (E); amalgamated<br>with 8th Hertfordshire Rifle<br>Volunteers retaining title 7th<br>Hertfordshire Rifle Volunteers 1 May<br>1866 | 11th Hertfordshire Rifle Volunteers<br>(Cheshunt)<br>Raised July 1860 (E); disbanded 22<br>November 1870 (partially absorbed into<br>22nd Essex R.V.) |
| 8th Hertfordshire Rifle Volunteers<br>(Tring)<br>Raised 20 April 1860 (E); amalgamated<br>with 7th Hertfordshire Rifle<br>Volunteers and designated 7th<br>Hertfordshire Rifle Volunteers 1 May<br>1866 | 12th Hertfordshire Rifle Volunteers<br>(Hitchin)<br>Raised 15 September 1860 (C); disbanded<br>27 February 1867 (but see 14th<br>Hertfordshire R.V.) |
| | 13th Hertfordshire Rifle Volunteers<br>(Watton-at-Stone)<br>Raised 8 September 1864 (C); disbanded 28<br>July 1868 |
| | 14th Hertfordshire Rifle Volunteers<br>(Welwyn and Hitchin)<br>1st Company (Welwyn) raised<br>26 August 1876<br>2nd Company (Hitchin) raised<br>7 November 1876 |
| | 22nd Essex Rifle Volunteers<br>(Waltham Abbey)<br>Raised 27 November 1860 (C); incorporated<br>in 2nd Administrative Battalion 1863;<br>partially absorbed 11th Hertfordshire R.V.<br>and designated 22nd Essex R.V. (Waltham<br>Abbey and Cheshunt) 1870 |

Note: The precedence of the individual corps within the county, and hence their numbered designations, was determined by reference to the dates of acceptance by the Queen of their offers to serve, which were submitted in accordance with regulations through the Lord Lieutenant. Acceptance was normally closely followed by enrolment, which often took place at an advertised public meeting. After enrolment officers were selected and their names were forwarded, again through the Lord Lieutenant, for appointment to commissions in the Volunteer Force, which were promulgated in the *London Gazette*. In no case has evidence of the date of acceptance of a Hertfordshire corps yet been traced. Accordingly, this table shows the earliest known date annotated as follows: date of enrolment (E), date of commission of the officer selected to command the corps (C).

basic similarity of uniform within the administrative battalions, minor differences persisted for several years. Style and cut varied, as did the colour of braid, but not that of facings, which were green for the 1st Administrative Battalion and scarlet for the 2nd. Badges also varied. The

TABLE 3.2  *Hertfordshire Rifle Volunteers 1880–1887*

*1st and 2nd Volunteer Battalions The Bedfordshire Regiment 1887–1908*

| | |
|---|---|
| 1st Hertfordshire Rifle Volunteer Corps<br>  later 1st Volunteer Battalion<br>Battalion Headquarters: Hertford<br><br>Uniform: Grey, facings scarlet<br>  later scarlet, facings white | 2nd Hertfordshire Rifle Volunteer Corps<br>  later 2nd Volunteer Battalion<br>Battalion Headquarters: Little Gaddesden<br>  later Hemel Hempstead<br>Uniform: Grey, facings green<br>  later grey, facings grey |
| A and B Companies    Hertford<br>(formerly 1st Hertfordshire R.V.) | A Company    Watford<br>(formerly 2nd Hertfordshire R.V.) |
| C Company    Bishop's Stortford<br>(formerly 6th Hertfordshire R.V.) | B Company    St. Albans<br>(formerly 3rd Hertfordshire R.V.) |
| D Company    Ware<br>(formerly 9th Hertfordshire R.V.) | C Company    Ashridge<br>(formerly 4th Hertfordshire R.V.) |
| E Company    Royston<br>(formerly 10th Hertfordshire R.V.) | D Company    Hemel Hempstead and<br>          Redbourn<br>(formerly 5th Hertfordshire R.V.) |
| F Company    Welwyn<br>(formerly part of 14th Hertfordshire<br>R.V.) | E Company    Berkhamsted and Tring<br>(formerly 7th Hertfordshire R.V.) |
| G Company    Hitchin<br>(formerly part of 14th Hertfordshire<br>R.V.) | F Company    Tring<br>(Raised by division of E Company 1883) |
| H Company    Waltham Abbey and<br>          Cheshunt<br>(formerly 22nd Essex R.V.) | G Company    Watford<br>(Raised by division of A Company July<br>1892) |
| I Company    Hoddesdon<br>(Raised 1900) | H Company    Dickinson's, Apsley<br>(Raised May 1900; disbanded January<br>1904) |

long tunic and French-inspired shako gave way to a shorter tunic worn with the home service pattern cloth helmet in the early 1870s. Thereafter badges were standardised within, but not between, battalions (later corps). A great variety of orders of dress were worn, as can be seen in the accompanying illustrations.

### 3.2  1st and 2nd (Hertfordshire) Volunteer Battalions The Bedfordshire Regiment 1887–1908

Under General Order 181 of December 1887, the three Rifle Volunteer Corps attached to the 16th Regimental District (as the 33rd Sub-District Brigade had become in 1881) were designated Volunteer battalions of the Bedfordshire Regiment, thus:

| | |
|---|---|
| 1st Hertfordshire Rifle<br>  Volunteer Corps | 1st (Hertfordshire)<br>  Volunteer Battalion |
| 2nd Hertfordshire Rifle<br>  Volunteer Corps | 2nd (Hertfordshire)<br>  Volunteer Battalion |
| 1st Bedfordshire Rifle<br>  Volunteer Corps | 3rd Volunteer Battalion |

There were no changes in the internal organisation or company designations of the two Hertfordshire battalions. Three additional companies, raised between 1887 and 1908, were lettered in sequence after existing companies, as can be seen in Table 3.2. At about this time the 2nd Volunteer Battalion's facings were changed from green to grey.

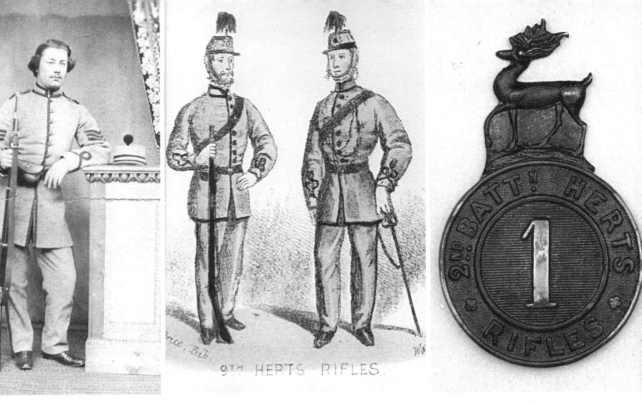

Figure 3.1 (Left)   *1st Hertfordshire (Hertford) Rifle Volunteers – A sergeant of the corps wearing the long-skirted tunic typical of the 1860s. He is holding the 'long' Enfield muzzle-loading rifle with which the Rifle Volunteers were first armed.*                    (Hertford Museum)
(Centre)   *9th Hertfordshire (Ware) Rifle Volunteers – Detail from a letter head showing a rifleman (left) and an officer (right) in the uniform worn soon after formation in 1860.*
(Hertfordshire County Record Office)
(Right)   *1st Hertfordshire (Hertford) Rifle Volunteers – Bronze finish headdress badge, c. 1865–70. (Actual size 43 mm. × 74 mm.)*                    (Hertford Museum)

Figure 3.2   *1st Hertfordshire (Hertford) Rifle Volunteers – Members of the corps in various orders of dress at Panshanger rifle range, 1868. Note the tall, 1855–61 pattern shakos.*
(Regimental collection)   [25]

Incorporation in the Bedfordshire Regiment did not entail any compulsion to adopt the scarlet tunic of the infantry of the line and the 2nd Volunteer Battalion continued to wear grey right up to the end of the Volunteer Force in 1908. The 1st Volunteer Battalion did opt to change, however, to the 'scarlet, facings white' of the Bedfordshire Regiment in 1897. It was a change in uniform only, though, for they continued to wear brown leather accoutrements rather than white, and both battalions drilled as rifles rather than infantry of the line.          (*Continued on page 45*)

Figure 3.3   *1st Hertfordshire (Hertford) Rifle Volunteers –
Rifleman, full dress, c. 1865. The grey uniform is relieved
by dark green lace, shoulder cords and plume and by red
facings at collar and cuff.*
(Water colour drawing by Reynolds, reproduced by
courtesy of the Board of Trustees of the Victoria and
Albert Museum)

Figure 3.4    *2nd Hertfordshire (Watford) Rifle Volunteers – The corps with their band in the early 1860s. Their simple grey uniform altered relatively little, except for changes in headdress, over nearly fifty years.*

(Watford Library)

Figure 3.5    *10th Hertfordshire (Royston and Baldock) Rifle Volunteers – (Left) An officer of the corps, c. 1875. His shako has a star plate with white metal hart similar to that shown in Figure 3.13 but the badge is not repeated on his pouch belt. (Right) – The Permanent Staff Instructor in the uniform of the corps, c. 1875. His medals are evidence of Regular service in the Crimea and in India.*

(Royston Museum)

Figure 3.6   *1st Hertfordshire (Hertford) Rifle Volunteers – The corps shooting team, winners of the Inland Revenue Cup, in 'informal undress', 1879.*

(Regimental collection)

Figure 3.7   *6th Hertfordshire (Bishop's Stortford) Rifle Volunteers – The corps, headed by their band, in North Street, Bishop's Stortford, c. 1880. Note the bandsmen's plumed helmets and frogged tunics.*

(J. D. Sainsbury)

Figure 3.8  *3rd Hertfordshire (St. Albans) Rifle Volunteers –* (Left) *White metal cross belt badge,* c. 1875. *(Actual size 55 mm. × 75 mm.)*                (Private collection)
*2nd Administrative Battalion Hertfordshire Rifle Volunteers –* (Centre) *Glengarry badge, bronze finish with polished 'highlights'. (Actual size 38 mm. × 65 mm.)* (Right) *Other ranks' white metal collar badge introduced in the early 1870s and worn until 1908. It was also used as a cap badge in the field service cap. (Actual size 27 mm. × 27 mm.)*
                (Hertford Museum)

Figure 3.9  *1st Hertfordshire (Hertford) Rifle Volunteers – A sergeant of the corps in full dress, drill order, late 1870s. He has the Snider breech-loading rifle with long, slightly curved sword bayonet, which was in general use between 1870 and the mid 1880s.*

                (Hertford Museum)

Figure 3.10  *2nd Administrative Battalion Hertfordshire Rifle Volunteers – (Left) Officer's helmet plate, 1879–1897. The white metal hart was exactly the same as that worn by the Hertfordshire Yeomanry Cavalry. The other ranks' star plate was bronze finished. (Actual size 113 mm. × 113 mm). (Right) Silver plate pouch belt badge. (Actual size 63 mm. × 74 mm.)*

(Hertford Museum)

Figure 3.11  *2nd Administrative Battalion Hertfordshire Rifle Volunteers – Officers and sergeants of the battalion (in grey uniforms) with officers and an honorary chaplain of the Essex Rifle Volunteers during exercises at Aldershot in 1879.*

(Hitchin Museum)

[30]

Figure 3.12  *2nd (Hertfordshire) Volunteer Battalion The Bedfordshire Regiment – (Left) Officer's helmet plate, white metal. (Actual size 102 mm. × 122 mm.) (Right) – Other ranks' helmet plate, white metal hart on bronze finish. (Actual size 105 mm. × 130 mm.)*

(J. D. Sainsbury)

Figure 3.13  *2nd (Hertfordshire) Volunteer Battalion The Bedfordshire Regiment – (Left) Pouch belt badge, white metal. (Actual size 55 mm. × 75 mm.)*

(J. D. Sainsbury)

*(Right) Officer's full dress belt clasp, silver-gilt. (Actual size 87 mm. × 47 mm.)*

(Private collection)  [31]

Figure 3.14 *2nd (Hertfordshire) Volunteer Battalion The Bedfordshire Regiment – (Left) Glengarry badge, white metal hart on highlighted bronze finish. (Actual size 33 mm. × 53 mm.)*

(Private collection)

(Centre) – *Collar badge, also worn on the slouch hat and the field service cap. Both white metal and brass versions were produced. (Actual size 45 mm. × 30 mm.)*

(Berkhamsted School)

(Right) – *White metal button, probably introduced in the 1860s, and worn until 1908. The 1st Volunteer Battalion used a button with 'a bugle, strung' and crown with their grey uniform, changing to the Royal Arms (for other ranks) and the Bedfordshire Regiment's button (for officers) when they adopted scarlet. (Diameter 24 mm.)*

(J. D. Sainsbury)

Figure 3.15 *2nd (Hertfordshire) Volunteer Battalion The Bedfordshire Regiment – A sergeant (left) and a sergeant-major instructor (seated) in informal undress with privates of the battalion in full dress, drill order, c. 1890.*

[32]

(Private collection)

Figure 3.16 (Left)   *2nd Hertfordshire Rifle Volunteer Corps – The medical officer taking part in the Golden Jubilee celebrations at Watford in 1887. Until 1908 local doctors were commissioned as surgeons in the Rifle Volunteers and wore the same uniform except that a black cocked hat replaced the normal full dress shako, or later, helmet. After 1908 medical officers were commissioned in the Royal Army Medical Corps and attached to Territorial units.*

(Watford Library)

(Right)   *1st (Hertfordshire) Volunteer Battalion The Bedfordshire Regiment – The officers of the battalion in various orders of dress, early 1890s.*

(J. D. Sainsbury)

Figure 3.17   *1st (Hertfordshire) Volunteer Battalion The Bedfordshire Regiment – The officers of the battalion in undress, field day order, with helmets, rolled greatcoats and haversacks, c. 1895. Both mounted and dismounted versions can be seen.*

(Hitchin Museum)   [33]

Figure 3.18    *1st (Hertfordshire) Volunteer Battalion The Bedfordshire Regiment – (Left) Silver plate pouch belt badge. (Actual size 60 mm. × 82 mm.) (Centre) Glengarry badge, bronze finish with white metal hart. (Actual size 38 mm. × 62 mm.) (Right) White metal badge, based on the badge of the Bedfordshire Regiment, worn on the field service cap and the Broderick cap (see Figure 3.32). (Actual size 40 mm. × 40 mm.)*

(Hertford Museum)

Figure 3.19    *1st (Hertfordshire) Volunteer Battalion The Bedfordshire Regiment – Field officer in full dress, mounted review order, early 1890s.*

[34]

(Regimental collection)

Figure 3.20    *1st (Hertfordshire) Volunteer Battalion The Bedfordshire Regiment – Other ranks of the battalion at camp, c. 1895. The field service cap with hart badge (Figure 3.8) has replaced the glengarry. Full dress, walking-out order and an informal undress worn off duty are shown.*

(J. D. Sainsbury)

Figure 3.21    *2nd (Hertfordshire) Volunteer Battalion The Bedfordshire Regiment – Shooting team in 'range undress', 1897. They are carrying bolt-action rifles – evidence that the .303-in. Lee-Metford had been issued to the battalion.*

(Private collection)    [35]

Figure 3.22   *1st (Hertfordshire) Volunteer Battalion The Bedfordshire Regiment – The Cyclist Section shortly after formation, c. 1893. The grey tunic with cartridge holders in place of the breast pockets was replaced quite shortly by the tunic and bandolier shown in Figure 3.23.*

(J. D. Sainsbury)

Figure 3.23   *1st (Hertfordshire) Volunteer Battalion The Bedfordshire Regiment – Members of the Cyclist Section in their distinctive uniform, c. 1896. The long socket bayonet for their Martini-Henry rifles, which replaced the Snider in the late 1880s, can be seen, especially at far right.*

(J. D. Sainsbury)

Figure 3.24  *1st (Hertfordshire) Volunteer Battalion The Bedfordshire Regiment – Subaltern officer's uniform as worn immediately before the change to scarlet, showing: (Left) full dress, review order; (Centre) full dress, informal order; (Right) undress.*  (Hertford Museum)

Figure 3.25  *1st (Hertfordshire) Volunteer Battalion The Bedfordshire Regiment – Assorted musicians at Hitchin, c. 1900. Three uniforms are shown: Bandsman's, with 'wings' (extreme left and right); bugler's with diced 'wings' and piping down sleeve seams (front, centre); and the normal private's uniform (centre, standing).*  (Hitchin Museum)

[37]

Figure 3.26   *1st (Hertfordshire) Volunteer Battalion The Bedfordshire Regiment – Some young privates of the battalion about to leave camp in full dress, walking-out order, c. 1900. The bolt-action Lee-Enfield rifle has replaced the Martini-Henry shown in Figures 3.32 and 3.33.*

(J. D. Sainsbury)

Figure 3.27 (Left)   *1st (Hertfordshire) Volunteer Battalion The Bedfordshire Regiment – The orderly officer, in undress, inspects the camp guard, in undress, guard order, c. 1900.*

(J. D. Sainsbury)

(Right)   *2nd (Hertfordshire) Volunteer Battalion The Bedfordshire Regiment – A private of H (John Dickinson's) Company in full dress, drill order, c. 1902. The grey uniform is embellished with piping and the hart trippant badge (Figure 3.14) is worn on the collar and on the field service cap. The brown leather belt is part of the Slade-Wallace infantry equipment and has attachments for the braces either side of the buckle.*

(A. J. Ward)

[38]

Plate 1

*Regimental Colour*

1st Battalion The Hertfordshire Regiment

*Presented by Her Majesty Queen Elizabeth The Queen Mother at Hertford on 25 October 1953; laid up in All Saints' Church, Hertford on 1 July 1967.*

(Specially drawn for this work by H. W. Gray, M.V.O.)

*Facing page 38*

Figure 3.28 *H Company (John Dickinson's), 2nd (Hertfordshire) Volunteer Battalion The Bedfordshire Regiment – the Company in full dress, drill order, c. 1902.*

(A. J. Ward)

Figure 3.29 *F (Welwyn) Company, 1st (Hertfordshire) Volunteer Battalion The Bedfordshire Regiment – A group of all ranks in full dress, c. 1902.*

(J. D. Sainsbury) [39]

Figure 3.30   *1st (Hertfordshire) Volunteer Battalion The Bedfordshire Regiment – Privates of the battalion at camp, probably 1900. They are wearing the scarlet undress tunic introduced at the turn of the century and readily distinguishable from full dress by the pockets at the waist and the absence of white piping down the front. (Compare with Figure 3.26.)*          (J. D. Sainsbury)

Figure 3.31   *1st (Hertfordshire) Volunteer Battalion The Bedfordshire Regiment – (Left) An officer in undress, mounted drill order, wearing the khaki field service hat (see also Figure 3.30) introduced in 1900.*          (J. D. Sainsbury)

[40]   *(Centre and right)   Two examples of officers' undress: the scarlet serge frock adopted in the late 1890s and the blue uniform which replaced it shortly afterwards.*          (Hertford Museum)

Figure 3.32   *1st (Hertfordshire) Volunteer Battalion The Bedfordshire Regiment – The Battalion Cyclist Section, c. 1900 (Top) and c. 1903 (Bottom). In keeping with their quasi-mounted role the cyclists wore bandoliers, rather than ammunition pouches, and knickerbocker breeches. The stockings and spats visible in the earlier photograph evidently gave way to orthodox blue puttees, as the field service cap did to the unpopular Broderick cap.*

(J. D. Sainsbury)   [41]

Figure 3.33  *1st (Hertfordshire) Volunteer Battalion The Bedfordshire Regiment – Members of E (Royston) Company with the battalion's Maxim machine-gun, c. 1903. They are all wearing khaki service dress but headgear varies between the slouch hat, the Broderick cap and the peaked service dress cap worn by the officer (right) and the permanent staff sergeant-major (behind gun).*

(Royston Museum)

Figure 3.34  *2nd (Hertfordshire) Volunteer Battalion The Bedfordshire Regiment – Field officer in undress, mounted drill order, c. 1905. Unusually, the 2nd Volunteer Battalion retained the slouch hat until 1908.*

[42]

(Regimental collection)

Figure 3.35   *2nd (Hertfordshire) Volunteer Battalion The Bedfordshire Regiment – The officers of the battalion in undress, drill order, c. 1905.* (J. D. Sainsbury)

Figure 3.36   *1st (Hertfordshire) Volunteer Battalion The Bedfordshire Regiment – The officers of E (Royston) Company c. 1903. Officers' khaki service dress with closed collar and bronze finish cap and collar badges was introduced in 1902. Note the mounted version of khaki service dress worn by the officer on the right, probably the battalion machine-gun officer.* (J. D. Sainsbury)   [43]

Figure 3.37 (Left)   *2nd (Hertfordshire) Volunteer Battalion The Bedfordshire Regiment – The battalion cyclist section at camp in 1904.*                          (Hitchin Museum)
(Right)   *1st (Hertfordshire) Volunteer Battalion The Bedfordshire Regiment – Officers and men wearing the khaki service dress with stiff-brimmed hat which was used for field training, and increasingly for other purposes, from 1902. The other ranks' embroidered white-on-red shoulder title 'BEDFORD-I-V' can be distinguished on the original photograph.*                          (J. D. Sainsbury)

Figure 3.38   *1st (Hertfordshire) Volunteer Battalion The Bedfordshire Regiment – Other ranks at camp in 1907, their last camp as members of the Volunteer Force. (Note that the full dress tunic now has pointed white cuffs, rather than the 'jam pot' cuff and Austrian knot, and that the scarlet sergeants' sash of the infantry of the line has replaced the leather pouch belts).*   (Hitchin Museum)

[44]

When volunteer infantry brigades were introduced in 1888 the two Hertfordshire battalions were included in the widespread Home Counties Volunteer Infantry Brigade, the other battalions of which were the 3rd Volunteer Battalion The Bedfordshire Regiment, 1st Buckinghamshire Rifle Volunteers, 2nd Volunteer Battalion The Oxfordshire Light Infantry and 1st Volunteer Battalion The Royal Berkshire Regiment. A more compact organisation was achieved in 1902, when the 1st, 2nd, and 3rd Volunteer Battalions The Bedfordshire Regiment were withdrawn from the Home Counties Brigade to form, with the newly-raised 4th (Huntingdonshire) Volunteer Battalion, the Bedford Volunteer Infantry Brigade.

The supply detachment of the Bedford Volunteer Infantry Brigade was at first found by the 3rd Volunteer Battalion. Early in 1904, however, supply and transport duties in support of the brigade were assumed by the brigade Army Service Corps company which was based at Royston and attached to 1st (Hertfordshire) Volunteer Battalion. It is probable that the company recruited throughout the brigade's three counties.

### 3.3  The Volunteer Active Service Companies 1900–1902

A total of 279 all ranks served in South Africa with the three successive volunteer active service companies that were attached to the 2nd Battalion The Bedfordshire Regiment between March 1900 and June 1902. Much the greater proportion of this total was provided by the two Hertfordshire battalions, which found 211 between them (1st Volunteer Battalion – 136; 2nd Volunteer Battalion – 75).

The first company, which, at 116 all ranks, was right up to the establishment laid down in Army Order 29 of 1900, assembled at Bedford in January 1900, sailed on 14 February and disembarked at Cape Town on 9 March. After some weeks of duty on the lines of communication the company joined the 2nd Battalion near Bloemfontein early in May and began outpost and convoy escort duties with the battalion almost at once. The Volunteer Company, which was reinforced by a draft of twenty-two all ranks in June, remained a separate sub-unit within the battalion. Most of the period May–August 1900 was spent in the area Winburg–Senekal–Bethlehem, to the north-east of Bloemfontein in the Orange River Colony, and was by nature tedious, however necessary. Actions at Naauwpoort Nek on 29 July and at Winberg on 26 August, in which the company took part, served to enliven the monotony. In September the company moved to Thaba'Nchu, immediately to the east of Bloemfontein, where it was to remain for a further seven months, most of which was spent on outpost duty. The company was ordered home on 1 April 1901 and finally reached Bedford, where they were given a most enthusiastic welcome, in mid-May.

Meanwhile, a second company, which at eighty-six all ranks was well short of full establishment, had assembled in February 1901 and reached South Africa early in April. On arrival the company moved immediately to join the 2nd Battalion at Thaba'Nchu, and remained on duty in that area for six weeks. They then moved east to Sanna's Post where they were based, securing the lines of communication eastward from Bloemfontein, for a further eight months.

The third, and last, company totalled only fifty-six all ranks and assembled at Bedford in January 1902, arriving in Cape Town on 9 March. The company joined the 2nd Battalion on 19 March and was at once deployed as blockhouse garrisons in the area of Brandford. During May

Figure 3.39 *Volunteer Active Service Company – A group of volunteers from Berkhamsted before departure for South Africa in 1900. They are wearing the khaki service uniform laid down in Army Order 29 of 1900 (and appear not yet to have mastered the art of applying their puttees, which had not previously been issued to Volunteer infantry). Conditions in South Africa quickly dictated a change from the white belts and rifle slings shown here to khaki.* (A. J. Ward)

the company spent some time on escort to ox-wagon convoys and on outpost duties. On 4 June peace was proclaimed and the company left South Africa on 24 June to return to England.

The services of the three active service companies earned for each of the parent Volunteer battalions the battle honour 'South Africa 1900–02', announced in a Special Army Order of 21 December 1904. One non-commissioned officer of 2nd Volunteer Battalion who served with the second company was mentioned in despatches and altogether eight men from the two Hertfordshire battalions lost their lives in South Africa. The worth of the Volunteers on active service was amply proved, albeit far from the homes they had originally enlisted to defend, and they were able now to look back with pride on their service (marked by the award of the Queen's South Africa Medal with appropriate clasps, depending on the period of service) and make good use of their experience.

[46]

# Chapter 4

# *The Hertfordshire Regiment 1908–1919*

## 4.1. 1st Battalion 1908–1914

The proposed order of battle of the Territorial Force in Hertfordshire provided for only one infantry battalion, to be formed by amalgamation of the 1st and 2nd Volunteer Battalions, which were, in addition, to provide the cadres for the 1st and 2nd Hertfordshire Batteries, Royal Field Artillery, new units being formed at Hertford/St. Albans and Watford/ Hemel Hempstead, respectively. The new battalion was to form part of the East Midland Infantry Brigade in the East Anglian Division. Army Council recognition as a newly constituted unit of the Territorial Force was not given until units had attested at least thirty per cent of their authorised establishment. The 1st Battalion lost no time in reaching this minimum and was recognised by an Army Council letter dated 15 May 1908 and notified in the first list of acceptances published as Army Order 131 of 1908.

It was some time before the title of the new battalion was agreed. The original War Office suggestion that the battalion should form part of the Bedfordshire Regiment with the designation '6th (Hertfordshire) Battalion' was unacceptable in Hertfordshire, particularly since the Hertfordshire battalion was senior to the Bedfordshire battalion, which was to be numbered 5th, even though formed from the 3rd Volunteer Battalion. Finally, after almost a year, during which it appeared in official records as the 'Hertfordshire Battalion', the unit was constituted as a regiment in its own right and took the designation 'Hertfordshire Regiment', the only battalion then raised becoming the 1st Battalion. Only two other infantry regiments of the Territorial Force were similarly formed by breaking from their former parent regiment – the Cambridgeshire Regiment from the 3rd Volunteer Battalion The Suffolk Regiment, and the 1st, 2nd and 3rd Battalions The Monmouthshire Regiment from the 2nd, 3rd and 4th Volunteer Battalions The South Wales Borderers. Approval of the regiment's title was announced in Army Order 67 published in March 1909.

The establishment for an infantry battalion of the Territorial Force was published as part of the blanket instructions for the raising of the Force detailed in Army Order 70 of 1908. It provided for battalion headquarters, eight rifle companies and a machine-gun section and totalled just over one thousand all ranks. The 1st Battalion The Hertfordshire Regiment was formed in accordance with this establishment from the 1st and 2nd Volunteer Battalions of the Bedfordshire Regiment as shown in Table 4.1.

As a new Territorial regiment of the infantry of the line the Hertfordshire Regiment conformed to the dress regulations for English non-royal regiments. There would have been no strong case for applying to do otherwise, and the 1st Volunteer Battalion had been wearing the prescribed 'uniform – scarlet; facings – white' for some years. The priority laid down in *Territorial Force Regulations* was for N.C.O.s and men to be provided [47]

TABLE 4.1   *Formation of 1st Battalion the Hertfordshire Regiment – 1908*

| 1st and 2nd Volunteer Battalions The Bedfordshire Regiment | 1st Battalion The Hertfordshire Regiment | |
|---|---|---|
| | Battalion Headquarters: Hertford | |
| A and B Companies 1st Volunteer Battalion | A Company Detachments | Hertford Watton, Little Berkhamsted |
| B Company 2nd Volunteer Battalion | B Company | St. Albans |
| C and D Companies 1st Volunteer Battalion | C Company Detachments | Bishop's Stortford Sawbridgeworth, Ware, Widford |
| A and G Companies 2nd Volunteer Battalion | D Company | Watford |
| F Company 1st Volunteer Battalion | E Company Detachments | Welwyn Hatfield, Stevenage |
| C, D, E and F Companies 2nd Volunteer Battalion | F Company Detachments | Hemel Hempstead Berkhamsted, Tring, Ivinghoe |
| E and G Companies 1st Volunteer Battalion | G Company Detachments | Hitchin Letchworth, Baldock, Royston, Ashwell |
| H and I Companies 1st Volunteer Battalion | H Company Detachments | Waltham Cross Hoddesdon, Wormley, Cheshunt |
| | Machine-Gun Section | Stevenage |
| | Corps of Drums | Ware |

with the approved pattern of khaki service dress. Only after one suit of service dress had been issued could commanding officers, in consultation with County Territorial Associations, arrange procurement of a walking-out uniform (not full dress) consisting of tunic, trousers and forage (peaked) cap. With the addition of the blue home service cloth helmet (which had been worn by the 1st Volunteer Battalion) and white leather belts (which were readily obtainable), the walking-out dress passed for full dress on the occasions (such as, for instance, the 1911 Coronation) when the wearing of full dress was authorised for those units which could outfit their representative parties. While the basic uniforms adopted by the Hertfordshire Regiment call for no comment, their choice of new badges is of interest. Both predecessor battalions had used the standing hart (the hart *trippant*, in heraldic terms) for many years on cap and collar. The new regiment chose to change to the kneeling hart (hart *lodged*) for reasons which do not seem to have been recorded but may have been to secure differentiation from the Bedfordshire Regiment which used the standing hart as a collar badge. The new badges are shown in Figure 4.2. Without any good historical grounds the Hertfordshire Regiment applied to the War Office for authority to wear a shoulder title based on the 'traditional' spelling of the county's name as 'Hartfordshire'. A trial title was actually made (Figure 4.2 *lower left*) but it was not approved and the spelling normally used at the time was adopted (Figure 4.2 *lower right*).

Infantry battalions of the Volunteer Force, which all traced their ancestry to local Rifle Volunteer Corps, had not been permitted to carry Colours. However, on transfer to the Territorial Force the situation changed, and *Territorial Force Regulations* provided for Territorial battalions other than

Figure 4.1   'The Hertfordshire Battalion' – Scenes at annual camp, the first as Territorials rather than Volunteers, in 1908. The khaki service dress cap which replaced the slouch hat and the Broderick cap, is being worn for the first time. The metal shoulder title T-HERTS has been issued but owing to the continuing dispute over the unit's title a Bedfordshire pattern cap badge is still being worn. Slade-Wallace pattern leather belts and pouches are still in use: they were shortly replaced by the 1908 Pattern Web Equipment.                                (J. D. Sainsbury)

Figure 4.2   The Hertfordshire Regiment – (Top left) Cap badge, made in bronze finish (later gilt) for officers and in gilding metal for other ranks, worn until 1961. (Actual size 27 mm. × 39 mm.). (Top centre) Collar badge, made in bronze finish (later gilt) for officers and gilding metal for other ranks, worn until 1961. (Actual size 35 mm. × 28 mm.) (Top right) Officer's gilt button worn until 1961. (Diameter 25 mm.) (Bottom left) The original design for the brass shoulder title, which the War Office rejected (see page 48) (Actual size 50 mm. × 25 mm.). (Bottom right) Other ranks' brass shoulder title introduced in 1908 and worn until 1939. (Actual size 50 mm. × 25 mm.)
                                                                                    (J. D. Sainsbury)     [49]

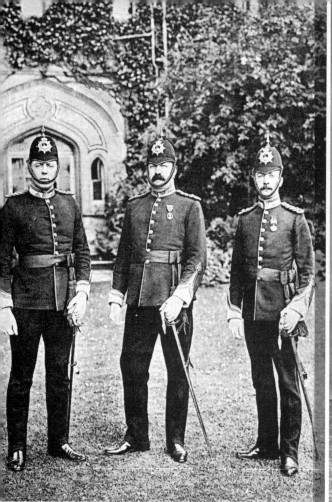

Figure 4.3  *1st Battalion The Hertfordshire Regiment – (Left) Officers in full dress, June 1909. The uniform is as laid down in Dress Regulations for officers of 'non-royal' regiments of English infantry with the addition of the regimental device – the hart 'lodged' – as helmet plate centre and collar badge, and regimental buttons.* (Hitchin Museum)
*(Right)   Other ranks' full dress, walking-out order (officially 'walking-out dress'), 1910. Comparison with Figure 3.26 will show that, in addition to the badges, the principal differences between this uniform and that of the 1st Volunteer Battalion were the pointed cuffs and the white piping round the shoulder strap. Additionally, the white pipeclayed belts and accoutrements of the Infantry of the Line replaced the Rifle Volunteers' brown leather.*

(J. D. Sainsbury)

those designated rifles to carry colours following the authorised patterns. The Sovereign's Colour was always based on the union flag, while Regimental Colours varied according to the facings of the regiment. As a unit with white facings the Hertfordshire Battalion was required to carry a Regimental Colour with the basic design of the red cross of St. George on a white ground. Regiments had for many years been permitted to place their 'Royal Badges or particular ancient badges' on their Colours and the Hertfordshire Battalion applied in October 1908 for the hart to be recognised as its 'ancient badge' for this purpose. The proposal was swiftly squashed and the Hertfordshire Territorial Association was told that the battalion 'must bear on its Colours the badge of the Bedfordshire Regiment, of which it forms part'. (As the Bedfordshire Regiment had not up to this time been authorised to bear an ancient badge on its Colours it would have been impossible to comply strictly with this instruction.) Once the battalion had been constituted as a regiment in its own right the matter

[50]

could properly be raised again and in April 1909 the King approved 'the design of a hart being adopted as a regimental badge to be borne on the Colour of The Hertfordshire Regiment'. Territorial units authorised to carry Colours were required to reach a strength equivalent to at least 75 per cent of their establishment before they received their Colours. At a huge parade at Windsor Castle on 19 June 1909 Guidons and Colours were presented to twelve Yeomanry regiments and ninety-six infantry battalions, including the 1st Battalion The Hertfordshire Regiment. The 1st Battalion's representative party brought the Colours back to Hertford, where they were at once paraded in the castle grounds (Figure 4.5). These Colours were eventually replaced by new ones (see later) and were laid up in All Saints' Church, Hertford in May 1954.

Regular infantry battalions were reorganised to a four-company establishment in October 1913 but this reform did not extend to the Territorial Force. Meanwhile, the layout of the 1st Battalion's company headquarters and drill stations originally adopted in 1908 did not prove entirely satisfactory and adjustments were made between 1908 and 1914. Thus it was with

Figure 4.4   *B (St. Albans) Company, The Hertfordshire Battalion – The company in 'full dress', 1908. Full dress was not authorised for other ranks of the Territorial Force but a passable imitation could be put together based on the authorised walking-out dress. In this photograph other ranks are wearing the scarlet walking-out dress tunic with pointed white cuff, as shown in Figure 4.3 (Right). They have all been provided, though possibly only temporarily, with the blue home service helmet, as worn by the 1st (Hertfordshire) Volunteer Battalion The Bedfordshire Regiment (see Figures 3.27 and 3.29). It is unfortunately not possible to distinguish the badge in the centre of the helmet plate but it may be assumed to be that of the Bedfordshire Regiment, perhaps with the addition of the designation 'Hertfordshire Battalion'. (It is known that such a plate was made but it is usually assumed to have been for trial purposes only.) White leather belts were normally worn by infantry of the line but they have not been issued to the company, who are wearing the brown belts from the Slade-Wallace infantry equipment used by both the earlier Volunteer battalions. The occasion on which this photograph was taken is not recorded but those tempted to suggest that it may in fact have been taken prior to 1908 should remember that the St. Albans company would then have been wearing the grey uniform of the 2nd Volunteer Battalion.*

(J. D. Sainsbury)

Figure 4.6    *1st Battalion The Hertfordshire Regiment – (Left) Officer, service dress, 1910. The 1902 pattern officers' service dress with closed collar and twisted shoulder cords was replaced in 1913 by a new pattern with open neck and shoulder straps. Badges of rank moved from the cuff to the shoulder strap during the First World War. (Right) Lance-corporal, service dress, c. 1910. The origin and extent of the practice of wearing the shoulder title on the collar remain a mystery. Although there is a record of official permission being given for this 'deviation' in 1921, it does not seem to have been put into effect after the First World War.*    (Watford Library)

the organisation shown in Table 4.2 that the battalion was mobilised in August 1914.

### 4.2    1st/1st Battalion 1914–1919

The battalion was at annual camp in Ashridge Park when it received orders to mobilise on 4 August 1914. It was thus well placed to complete mobilisation procedures swiftly and move with the rest of the East Midland Infantry Brigade to war stations in East Anglia. A sufficient proportion of the battalion volunteered for 'Imperial Service' when invited to do so and the battalion was earmarked for service abroad when a suitable opportunity arose. Meanwhile, former members were re-enlisted and

Figure 4.5 (on facing page)    *1st Battalion The Hertfordshire Regiment – The Colour Party with the newly presented Colours at Hertford Castle, June 1909. The presentation of Colours at Windsor was one of the few occasions on which other ranks wore full dress, including the spiked helmet, before the outbreak of war in 1914.*    (Hitchin Museum)    [53]

TABLE 4.2   *1st Battalion the Hertfordshire Regiment – 1914*

| | |
|---|---|
| Battalion Headquarters | Hertford |
| A Company<br>    Detachment | Hertford<br>    Hatfield |
| B Company | St. Albans |
| C Company<br>    Detachments | Bishop's Stortford<br>    Ware, Widford,<br>    The Hadhams, Braughing |
| D Company | Watford |
| E Company | Royston |
| F Company<br>    Detachments | Hemel Hempstead<br>    Berkhamsted, Tring, Ashridge |
| G Company<br>    Detachments | Hitchin<br>    Stevenage, Welwyn, Whitwell |
| H Company<br>    Detachments | Waltham Cross<br>    Cheshunt, Wormley, Hoddesdon |
| Machine-Gun Section | Stevenage |
| Corps of Drums | Ware |

preparations made to receive and train recruits – a task shortly to be taken over by the Depot and the Reserve battalion (see below).

It had been expected that Territorial units would get at least six months' training after embodiment and before being committed to action. The 1st Battalion barely had the opportunity of three months, however, before being numbered amongst the first three Territorial battalions selected to join the British Expeditionary Force in France. They left Bury St. Edmunds, where they had been in billets for some time, on 5 November 1914 and sailed from Southampton, arriving at Le Havre early on 6 November. Having mobilised with the 'long' Lee-Enfield .303-in. rifle, it was not until two days before sailing that the battalion was issued with the 'short' (No. 3) Lee-Enfield and it does look, from available records, as if men may have gone into action with weapons they had not previously fired. There is certainly no evidence that zeroing was carried out, possibly because it was believed there would be time for further training in France. In fact the German advance in Flanders had not yet been halted and the battalion was moved into the Ypres sector where the First Battle of Ypres was already in progress. They first went into the forward area and came under shell fire on 11 November and that day qualified for their first battle honour of the First World War – 'Nonne Bosschen', a subsidiary action of First Ypres – while employed in the preparation of entrenched defences behind the front line. On 20 November 1914 the battalion joined 4 Guards Brigade of 2nd Infantry Division, after which they spent a month refitting and training at Méteren, south-west of Ypres.

In January 1915 the battalion, which had mobilised on the old eight-company establishment was, in common with other Territorial battalions, reorganised on to the four-company establishment. As a line battalion brigaded with three Guards battalions it is not surprising that the 1st Battalion The Hertfordshire Regiment numbered its new companies. No. 1 Company was formed from A and H Companies, No. 2 Company from B and F Companies, No. 3 Company from C and D Companies and No. 4 Company from E and G Companies. From this time until amalgamation in 1961 (see later) the Hertfordshire Regiment numbered its companies

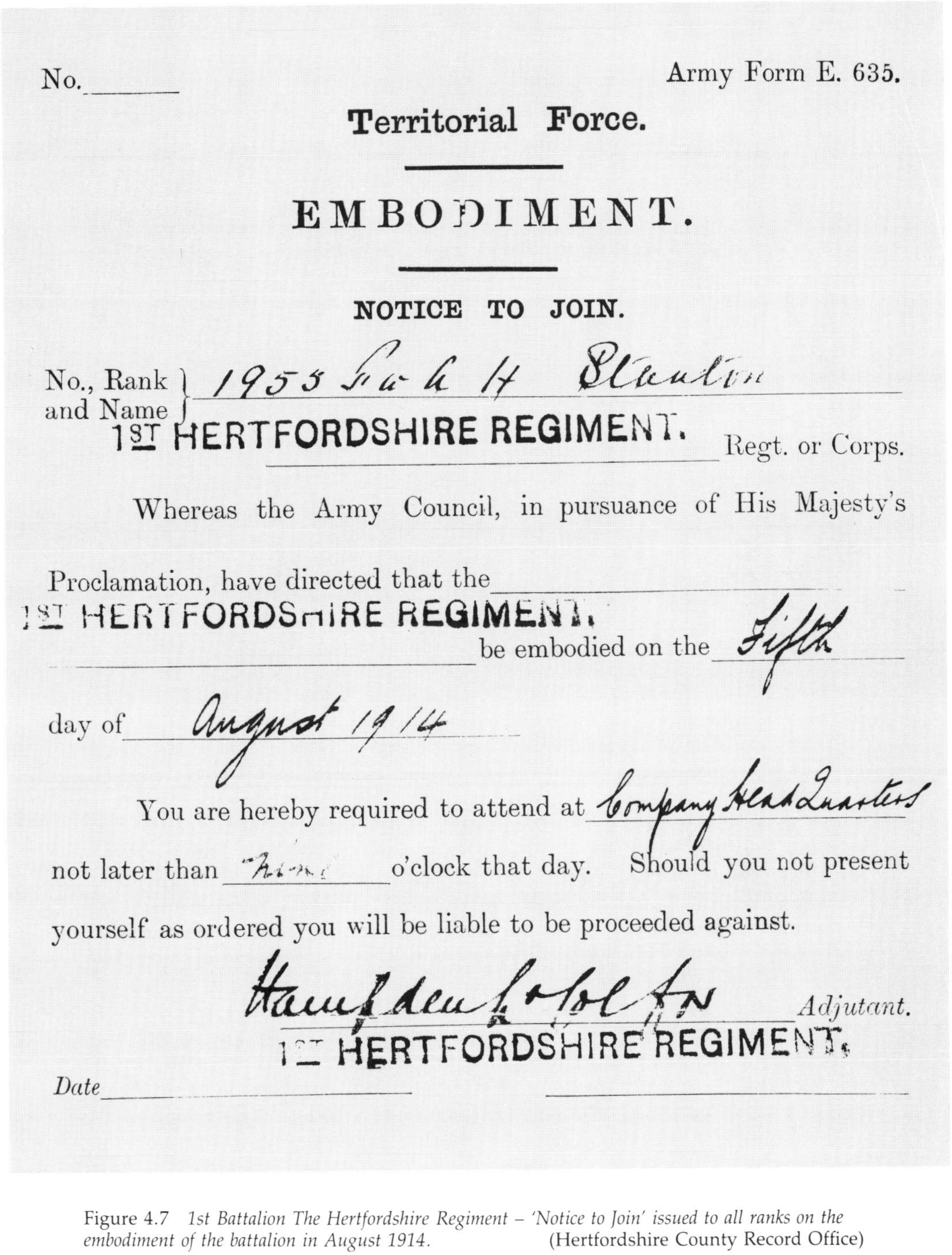

No. _____                                            Army Form E. 635.

## Territorial Force.

## EMBODIMENT.

### NOTICE TO JOIN.

No., Rank ⎫  *1955 Sick h H Stanton*
and Name ⎭ _____
**1ST HERTFORDSHIRE REGIMENT.**   Regt. or Corps.

Whereas the Army Council, in pursuance of His Majesty's

Proclamation, have directed that the _____
**1ST HERTFORDSHIRE REGIMENT.**
_____ be embodied on the _*Fifth*_

day of _*August 1914*_____

You are hereby required to attend at _*Company Head Quarters*_

not later than _*Nine*_____ o'clock that day.  Should you not present

yourself as ordered you will be liable to be proceeded against.

*Hampden C Colston*          *Adjutant.*
**1ST HERTFORDSHIRE REGIMENT,**

Date _____          _____

Figure 4.7   *1st Battalion The Hertfordshire Regiment – 'Notice to Join' issued to all ranks on the embodiment of the battalion in August 1914.*          (Hertfordshire County Record Office)

Figure 4.8 (Left)   *Colonel Sir Charles Longmore, K.C.B., V.D., T.D. (1855–1930) – First commissioned in the 1st Hertfordshire (Hertford) Rifle Volunteers 1874; Commanding Officer 1st (Hertfordshire) Volunteer Battalion The Bedfordshire Regiment 1900–08, 1st Battalion The Hertfordshire Regiment 1908–13 and 2nd/1st Battalion 1914–16; Honorary Colonel 1921–30.*
(Right)   *Brigadier-General Viscount Hampden, G.C.V.O., K.C.B., C.M.G. (1869–1958) – Commanding Officer, 1st Battalion The Hertfordshire Regiment 1913–14; Honorary Colonel 1930–47.*

and this tradition has been continued by its successor units. Also in January 1915 the battalion was designated 1st/1st Battalion The Hertford-shire Regiment in conformity with the arrangements for distinguishing between '1st-line' and reserve or training units. Lieutenant-Colonel Viscount Hampden, under whose command the battalion had mobilised and seen its first action, left on promotion to the command of a brigade in January and was succeeded by Lieutenant-Colonel H. Page Croft.

It was by now clear that forecasts that the war would be 'over by Christmas' had been wrong and the battalion settled down to what was to become a four-year struggle against the appalling conditions of winters on the Western Front and against horrifying bombardment by high explosive and gas shell, the constant threat of enemy sniping and raids, and sometimes sheer boredom. Full-scale battles, either offensive or defensive, took place only intermittently but it is generally these that stand out in the war diary and in personal letters and memoires.

The battalion's first offensive action was on 6 February 1915 when 4 Guards Brigade attacked successfully in the area of Cuinchy Brickstacks, east of Béthune. By later standards this would be judged a small affair, but Nos. 2 and 3 Companies' decisive action in support of the two leading battalions on 6 February and during the enemy counter-attack the following day contributed to a steady build-up of the regard in which the 1st Battalion was held, first in 4 Guards Brigade and later in all subsequent formations with which it served. The battalion attracted further attention for its fine work in trench digging in the face of considerable opposition during the preparations for the British offensive at Neuve Chapelle in March 1915. At the Battle of Festubert in May 1915 the battalion had its first experience of large-scale casualties but succeeded in gaining valuable ground.

In August 1915 1st/1st Battalion The Hertfordshire Regiment was replaced in 4 Guards Brigade by the newly formed 1st Battalion The Welsh Guards and was transferred to 6 Infantry Brigade – still in 2nd Infantry Division. The Battle of Loos opened on 25 September 1915 and found the 1st Battalion in support of the 6 Brigade attack eastwards from Cuinchy. The initial attack failed and the battalion was not called on to advance. The following day they took over the front line and would have been one of the leading battalions when the attack was resumed on 27 September. However, patrols ascertained that a preliminary attack by gas had not immobilised the enemy and the battalion was once again ordered not to advance. It was while the battalion was waiting to go 'over the top' on 27 September that Corporal A. A. Burt of Hertford performed an act of great individual bravery for which he was subsequently awarded the battalion's first Victoria Cross. The citation recorded his deed as follows:

> His company had lined the front trench preparatory to an attack when a large minenwerfer bomb [a heavy mortar bomb] fell into the trench. Corporal Burt, who knew well the destructive power of these bombs, might easily have taken cover behind a traverse but he immediately went forward, put his foot on the fuse, wrenched it out of the bomb and threw it over the parapet, thus rendering the bomb innocuous. His presence of mind and great pluck saved the lives of others in the traverse.

The Battle of Loos continued for a further ten days, much of which the battalion spent in the line, but without being involved in further attempts to advance.

Loos was followed, as far as the 1st Battalion was concerned, by about nine months of relative inactivity. Early in February 1916 Lieutenant-Colonel H. Page Croft handed over command to Lieutenant-Colonel F. Page and later the same month the battalion was transferred from 6 Brigade to 118 Brigade of 39th Infantry Division, the formation in which it was to serve for the next two years. The succession of actions now known collectively as the Battles of the Somme began on 1 July 1916 and continued for more than four months. The battalion was not directly involved in the early stages. During August 39th Division was withdrawn from the area east of Béthune and marched south by stages, spending some time training on the way. By the end of the month they had reached their intended area of operations west of Thiepval. A divisional attack north-west of the River Ancre on 3 September, in which 118 Brigade was in reserve, failed. The rest of the month was spent securing the line, with the battalion employed for the most part in repairing trenches and dug-outs and providing working parties for the transport of ammunition and other necessaries of war, including duck-boards, into the forward areas. Throughout October and the first few days of November 1916 39th Division operated to secure its part of the start line for the eventual attack north-westwards across the Ancre. This included the capture of the 'Schwaben Redoubt', a phased action in which a single platoon of the 1st Battalion played a distinguished part on 14 October. These operations, known as the Battle for the Ancre Heights, were largely complete on 39th Division's front by the end of October and preparations were made for the Battle of the Ancre, which opened on 13 November.

Figure 4.9 (Left)   *Brigadier-General H. P. Croft, C.M.G., T.D. (subsequently Lord Croft; 1881–1947) – First commissioned in the 1st (Hertfordshire) Volunteer Battalion The Bedfordshire Regiment 1900; Commanding Officer, 1st Battalion The Hertfordshire Regiment 1914–15 and 1920–24.*
(Right)   *Corporal A. A. Burt, V.C. – 'His presence of mind and great pluck saved the lives of others . . .'*

The 1st Battalion, as the right flank battalion of 118 Brigade, played an outstanding part in the opening stages of the battle, when, advancing northwards from the Schwaben Redoubt, behind a 'perfect' barrage before dawn and through mist, they progressively captured all their objectives, including about a thousand yards of the enemy's 'Hansa Line', and established a new front line resting on the Ancre. Despite the difficulties of darkness and fog and the appalling state of the ground over which they had to advance, the battalion succeeded in keeping direction and suffered minimal losses. The enemy attempted to regain lost ground by a counter-attack against the new front line but were successfully beaten off. The battalion was relieved after more than forty-eight hours' continuous action.

At the end of November 1916 39th Division moved back to the Ypres sector. The following seven months were uneventful, with the battalion alternating spells in the front line with periods in reserve, much of the latter occupied in building and maintaining the railway network in the rear areas. For ten days in July 1917 the 1st Battalion, in common with other units due to lead the assault at the opening of the Third Battle of Ypres, went through special training in offensive tactics and detailed rehearsals. The battle began at 03.50 on 31 July 1917, with 39th Division advancing from the line of the canal north of Ypres in a north-easterly direction on to the 'Pilckem Ridge' and beyond. Thorough artillery preparation and a rolling barrage in front of the assault waves enabled 116 and 117 Brigades to capture their objectives and pass 118 Brigade through for the third phase of the attack, which began at about 09.00.

The battalion had much to contend with after leaving their start line. The planned artillery barrage did not materialise and two tanks allocated to the support of the battalion failed to cross the Steenbeek brook some five hundred yards beyond the start line. The battalion pressed on, nevertheless, up the rising ground beyond the Steenbeek and through the village of St. Julien which lay on the right of their advance, capturing a battery of German artillery in so doing. The 1st Battalion were in the centre of the brigade and although they were in touch with the right-hand battalion they had lost contact with the left. It was from this flank that they came under persistent fire from machine-guns in pill boxes, which caused some casualties. In the midst of these difficulties the enemy launched a counter-attack supported by two aircraft. This was beaten off, largely thanks to No. 1 Company, on the battalion's right. In the face of intense rifle and machine-gun fire the battalion continued to advance and small parties actually reached their objective, despite the strongly wired defences. They were, however, in insufficient strength to make any lodgement and the brigade reserve, even assuming they knew of the difficulties at the front, would have been prevented from intervening by well placed defensive artillery fire. Unable to secure its toehold on the third objective, 118 Brigade fell back during the afternoon and by nightfall had withdrawn to the general line of the Steenbeek brook.

The day had been a devastating one for the 1st Battalion. The commanding officer, Lieutenant-Colonel F. Page, D.S.O. and ten officers were killed, and more than 130 men. All the remaining officers and more than two hundred men were wounded, and the 130 or so of the battalion who were still fit for duty finished the day under the command of the regimental sergeant-major, ably assisted by the padre. Following these huge losses the battalion took some time to regain its fighting strength. Lieutenant-Colonel E.C.M. Phillips was appointed to command and drafts joined throughout August and early September so that by the time the Battle of the Menin Road (part of the Third Battle of Ypres) opened on 20 September 1917 the battalion was again ready for action. They did not take any leading part in this action but simply while holding newly-won positions suffered over two hundred casualties from hostile shelling. Though credited with honours for subsequent actions in the Third Battle of Ypres the battalion in fact played relatively little part in them.

At the end of January 1918 39th Division left the Ypres sector and moved south to the area immediately east of Amiens. In February the 1st Battalion was transferred within 39th Division from 118 Brigade to 116 Brigade. When the German offensive in Picardy began on 21 March 39th Division was in G.H.Q. reserve. Early pressure on VII Corps front led to the division being released to support VII Corps and 116 Brigade was placed temporarily under command of 16th Division. The brigade went into the line on the evening of 21 March between Epéhy and Ste. Emilie, north-west of St. Quentin. During 16th Division's withdrawal the following day (22 March) the 1st Battalion, as rearguard battalion of 116 Brigade, was heavily engaged throughout the day and suffered considerable casualties. One company was cut off in the hamlet of Ste. Emilie and held up the enemy advance for a further valuable two hours before being overcome. During the night of 22–23 March 116 Brigade reverted to command of 39th Division and was sent back to prepare a further defensive line at Bussu, some five miles to the rear of the existing front line, on to which the division retired on the morning of the 23rd.

Enemy pressure was such that a further retirement was ordered in the early afternoon of 23 March. The rearguard was again undertaken by 116 Brigade and the battalion made a fighting withdrawal through the area of Mont St. Quentin to establish a defensive perimeter in front of Cléry-sur-Somme, an important crossing point. This position, part of a line held by 116 Brigade, which was the only brigade of 39th Division north of the Somme, was maintained overnight but a brisk attack on the morning of 24 March forced back 21st Division, to which 116 Brigade was temporarily attached, and left the brigade yet again in rearguard position. During the confused fighting that ensued throughout the day the commanding officer of the 1st Battalion, Lieutenant-Colonel E.C.M. Phillips, was captured. The fighting withdrawal continued on the morning of 25 March. Later in the day 116 Brigade disengaged and moved south across the Somme to rejoin 39th Division as divisional reserve, some six miles behind the two forward brigades. The enemy attacked again on the morning of 26 March and forced 118 Brigade to give ground. Another full day of fighting withdrawal followed, with 116 Brigade being deployed forward to allow 117 and 118 Brigades to withdraw through their position. The 'leap-frog' continued until nightfall, at which time 116 Brigade were yet again in divisional reserve.

The 1st Battalion was by now very severely depleted. Major A.G. Clerk, who had assumed command when Lieutenant-Colonel Phillips had been captured, was for a time commanding the remnants of 116 Brigade and the battalion, with only three officers remaining, was fielding three companies which cannot have had a fighting strength of more than about one normal platoon each. The German attack along 39th Division's front at dawn on 27 March was 'faint hearted' (according to battalion records) and made no headway. However, the enemy did make progress against 16th Division, holding the line between the left flank of 39th Division and the River Somme. During the day 116 Brigade moved to face north and a counter-attack by the 1st Battalion forced the enemy to retire on Morcourt. Nevertheless, by early evening the division was all but surrounded, so much so that on that evening alone during the retreat the transport failed to get through to bring rations and water to the exhausted remnants of the battalion.

Positions were held throughout the night and the withdrawal, now in a southerly, rather than westerly, direction resumed during the morning of 28 March, when a temporary line was established facing north across the River Luce near Cayeux. Each brigade of 39th Division was by now reduced to operating as a single weak battalion. Despite their weakened state these brigade-battalions carried out two counter-attacks during the day with the intention of driving the enemy north so that he did not have direct observation over the Luce valley. These attacks were partially successful and 39th Division held its rather exposed position until ordered to withdraw westwards on to Aubercourt during the night. The division was now reduced to about seven hundred fit officers and men.

By the standards of the previous few days 29 March was 'quiet' and in the evening the division was withdrawn into a support position to the west of Aubercourt. Early in the morning of 30 March troops from the forward line were seen withdrawing towards the support line. These stragglers were gathered and 39th Division organised two counter-attacks during the afternoon. By evening the division had, as had neighbouring formations, reached the point where it was totally exhausted and ineffective.

Fortunately fresh troops had now arrived, in the shape of 9th Australian Brigade which assembled behind 39th Division. Their counter-attacks, with troops of the 1st Cavalry Division, began during the afternoon of 30 March and marked the end of the German advance. During the night of 30–31 March the battered 39th Division was relieved and the remnants of the 1st Battalion were brought out of the line and into billets near Amiens. For ten days the battalion had fought continuously, opposing the enemy throughout a withdrawal of more than thirty miles, losing almost all its fighting strength in the process. The Battles Nomenclature Committee felt unable to distinguish between the many subsidiary actions of the retreat, giving them the overall title 'First Battles of the Somme, 1918'. Two component battles – 'St. Quentin' (21–23 March) and 'Rosières' (26–27 March) – were also recognised. The 1st Battalion was subsequently awarded all three; none were better earned.

The first few days of April 1918 were spent reorganising and re-equipping, no doubt in the expectation that the battalion would regain its full strength and return to operations after a period of training. This was not to be. No sooner had the enemy offensive in Picardy been halted (officially on 5 April) than another was opened, on 9 April, in Flanders. On 10 April orders were issued for 39th Division to reorganise to form a single brigade, known as 39 Composite Brigade, consisting of four composite battalions. No. 1 Composite Battalion was to be formed from the 1st Battalion, which provided two companies, and the 11th Battalion The Royal Sussex Regiment – an original 116 Brigade unit. On 1 April the composite battalion moved into the G.H.Q. support line immediately south of Ypres and spent the next week working on the defences, with occasional interference by enemy shelling, sometimes heavy, and air attack. The enemy attacked across the Wytschaete ridge on the morning of 24 April and had broken through to the battalion's positions by 21.00 but they were held. At dawn on 25 April the attack was resumed after a fierce bombardment with high explosive and gas shell and the battalion front was penetrated between the two forward companies, both of which withdrew fighting. The ground lost was recovered by immediate counter-attack and during the day the situation was stabilised. The battalion remained in the line for three more days, until the night of 28–29 April. Although the enemy kept up continuous heavy bombardment of the front held by the battalion, there was no further attack. The April offensive in Flanders, known later as the Battles of the Lys, had been halted.

Reorganising and re-equipping were resumed at the beginning of May. On 9 May 1st/1st Battalion The Hertfordshire Regiment left 39th Division and moved south to the area between Arras and Amiens on transfer to 112 Brigade of 37th Division, which they reached on 11 May. While the battalion was moving up into the line near Foncquevillers on the evening of 11 May it was subjected to very heavy bombardment with gas shell and, except for transport and rear details, sustained one hundred per cent casualties. This was the third time that the battalion had ceased to exist as an effective fighting unit and it is remarkable, given the very difficult manpower situation in the spring of 1918, that it was reconstituted. Its high reputation and the fact that it was now the sole representative unit of the Hertfordshire Regiment probably both told with the authorities and a huge new infusion of officers and men (thirty and 650 repectively) was found from the 6th (Service) Battalion The Bedfordshire Regiment, which was reducing to training cadre. Major R.C. Carthew, M.C., of the Essex Regiment, was appointed to command the battalion and shortly promoted lieutenant-colonel. The title, and to some extent the spirit, of the battalion were thus saved, and largely by men from the same district, but it is probably true to say that the 1st Battalion was never quite the same as the old 'Herts Guards'. After a month largely devoted to training, the battalion moved back into the same reserve trenches east of Foncquevillers that it had been intended to occupy on 11 May. Late July and early August 1918 were very quiet, with the battalion alternating spells of duty in the front line and in reserve.

The opening stages of 'The Advance to Victory' (as it was later known) began immediately east of Amiens on 8 August. On 21 August 37th Division attacked eastward from Bucquoy with 111 Brigade leading and 112 Brigade, including the 1st Battalion, providing carrying parties and working parties to rebuild captured strongpoints. The next day was spent resting and moving into position for the division's attack, with 111 and 112 Brigades 'up', on Achiet-le-Grand on 23 August. This attack began well at 11.00 but 112 Brigade got into some difficulty to the south of the village. The battalion lost direction (and, the Official History implies, cohesion, because it was 'full of new officers and men who did not know each other, under a recently arrived lieutenant-colonel') and moved too far south, striking the general line of the objective – a heavily defended railway cutting – in the neighbouring battalion's area. The village of Achiet-le-Grand was occupied but not all the day's objectives were attained. During the evening of 23 August an attempt was made by 63 and 112 Brigades to secure the remaining objectives and exploit forward towards the Arras–Bapaume road. This attack was met by very heavy fire from well dug-in and concealed machine guns and was abandoned after the battalion had sustained a considerable number of casualties. (Their total for the day, killed and wounded, was 175.) The following day 112 Brigade went into divisional reserve and the battalion spent several days training, returning to the front line on 3 September near Vélu, east of Bapaume.

The advance was resumed, with 112 Brigade leading, along the general line of the Canal du Nord towards Havrincourt on 4 September. This proved a difficult day and with no artillery support the leading battalions, including the 1st Battalion, did not make great progress. The following day Lieutenant-Colonel J.L. Heselton, D.S.O., M.C., of the Worcestershire Regiment took over command of the battalion. There was little further activity, other than following up where possible the enemy's withdrawal, until the opening of the Battle of Havrincourt on 12 September – the first stage in the assault on the 'Hindenburg Line' – during which 112 Brigade were in support. The battalion occupied the front-line positions during the night of 15–16 September and led the resumed advance into the Hindenburg Line on 18 September. The enemy's counter-attack that same evening recovered some of his lost ground and it was in its, largely successful, efforts to repel this counter-attack that the battalion gained its second Victoria Cross. Second-Lieutenant F.E. Young, seeing that the enemy had captured one of the forward companies' posts, led a counter-attack which cleared the post of the enemy. He was captured but escaped shortly afterwards, having knocked down two of the enemy with his fists. Returning to the battalion lines he organised and led a second counter-attack and was last seen in the thick of hand-to-hand fighting. His posthumous Victoria Cross was gazetted on 14 December 1918 with the following citation:

Figure 4.10 (Left) *Lieutenant-Colonel F. Page, D.S.O. (Killed in action 31 July 1917) – First commissioned in the 1st (Hertfordshire) Volunteer Battalion The Bedfordshire Regiment 1901 after service in the ranks; Commanding Officer 1st/1st Battalion The Hertfordshire Regiment February 1916 – July 1917.*
(Right) *2nd Lieutenant F. E. Young, V.C. (Killed in action 18 September 1918) – 'Throughout four hours of intense hand-to-hand fighting 2nd Lieutenant Young displayed the utmost valour and devotion to duty'.*

For most conspicuous bravery, determination and exceptional devotion to duty on 18th September 1918, south-east of Havrincourt, when, during an enemy counter-attack, and throughout an extremely intense barrage, he visited all posts, warned the garrisons, and encouraged the men. In the early stages of the attack he rescued two of his men who had been captured, and bombed and silenced an enemy machine-gun. Although surrounded by the enemy, Second-Lieutenant Young fought his way back to the main barricade and drove out a party of the enemy who were assembling there. By his further exertions the battalion was able to maintain a line of great tactical value, the loss of which would have meant serious delay to future operations. Throughout four hours of intense hand-to-hand fighting Second-Lieutenant Young displayed the utmost valour and devotion to duty, and set an example to which the company gallantly responded. He was last seen fighting hand-to-hand against a considerable number of the enemy.

[63]

The battalion was relieved on 19 September and spent the rest of the month in reserve, taking no part in the crossing of the Canal du Nord and the St. Quentin Canal, which were secured by 2 October. The battle to recapture Cambrai opened on 8 October with 37th Division amongst the forward divisions. After a night approach march 112 Brigade passed through 111 Brigade, which had attacked before dawn, the battalion leading the advance through Brisieux Wood, which they cleared after some three hours fighting. Two further days of fighting, in which the battalion played a full part, pressed the enemy back across the River Selle, which the leading company crossed on 12 October. On the night of 12–13 October 37th Division was withdrawn to reserve and did not return to the attack until 23 October. The final advance in Picardy had begun on 17 October and the Battle of the Selle was well under way when 112 Brigade led the attack towards Ghissignies before dawn on 24 October. The day turned out to be a difficult one. The leading battalions (1st/1st Hertford-shire Regiment and 13th Royal Fusiliers) were considerably delayed by congestion of the roads and heavy shelling during the approach, in dark-ness, to the start line. The battalion fell behind the barrage and were threatened with even greater disruption of timings when they encountered strong belts of wire. They managed to catch up, however, only to be halted by very heavy fire from Salesches railway station which had been turned into a strong point. Bitter fighting ensued before the area was secured and some fifty of the enemy were captured, together with more than twenty machine-guns and a complete 8-inch howitzer. The brigade was then overlooking the objective – the village of Ghissignies and the crossings of the River Écaillon. All further attempts to advance were frus-trated by heavy fire from well sited machine-guns covering the enemy's defensive line along the railway north-east of the village. The battalion's last attempt that night was at 21.00 hours but after gaining a toe-hold the two leading companies were forced back. The attack was resumed at 10.00 hours on 25 October after a heavy bombardment, but was again held up by very heavy enfilade fire from machine-guns on both flanks and by mortar fire. No progress was made before the battalion came out of the line on 27 October after some two days of heavy bombardment with a high proportion of gas, which was particularly suited to the combination of ground and weather.

The advance was resumed on the morning of 4 November, with 37th Division attacking eastwards from Ghissignies through Louvignies and into the Forêt de Mormal. The first two objectives, which included the railway line that had given so much trouble earlier, fell to 111 Brigade after heavy fighting. Soon after 09.00 hours 112 Brigade took over the lead. The country was close, greatly favouring the enemy's defence, and resistance was stubborn, relying to a great extent on well concealed mach-ine-guns, which were in some numbers. By about mid-day, however, steady pressure from the leading battalions, which included 1st/1st Hert-fordshire, forced the enemy's retirement and all the brigade's objectives were secured before dark. On the following day, 5 November, four years to the day after they had sailed for France, the battalion was withdrawn to reserve positions and did not return to the front line before the cease-fire on 11 November.

The battalion spent the six weeks following the Armistice on the move, with halts of a few days in towns and villages in Northern France, until arriving on 20 December 1918 at Ransart, near Charleroi in Belgium, where they remained in billets for some four months. On 11 December the battalion's Colours, which had been in safe-keeping in All Saints' Church, Hertford throughout the war, arrived from England and all ranks settled down to a peace-time routine while demobilisation proceeded. From a strength of well over nine hundred all ranks in mid-November the battalion had sunk to seven hundred by the end of January 1919, and by early March, when Lieutenant-Colonel Heselton relinquished command, numbers were such that it could be reorganised into only two companies. A representative cadre of four officers and fifty other ranks returned to the United Kingdom, with the Colours, on 20 April 1919 but, regrettably, was dispersed without returning formally to Hertford. The 1st/1st Battalion's war was at last over, and few wanted immediately to give any thought to its survival during the new peace.

### 4.3   War-formed Battalions and the Depot 1914–1917

The raising of additional units of the Territorial Force to take the place within the United Kingdom defences of units that had volunteered for 'Imperial Service', and to provide a training organisation, was first authorised in August 1914.[1] The precise role of these units, their designations and the arrangements for their administration evolved, not without some confusion, over the following seven months.[2]

Each Territorial infantry battalion abroad was to be backed by two battalions at home. The 'second-line' battalion, composed mainly of men fit for Imperial Service, was to take the 'first-line' battalion's place in the United Kingdom defences. Second-line battalions were formed in September 1914 and known initially as 'Reserve' battalions. They were redesignated '1st Reserve' in November 1914 and from the end of January 1915 their second-line status was shown by 2/ in front of the title of the original unit, the first-line battalion having 1/ (see page 56).

'Third-line' units, originally known as '2nd Reserve', and from the end of January 1915 carrying 3/ in front of their original title, were authorised in November 1914 to be raised 'when an Imperial Service unit has proceeded abroad to join the Expeditionary Force and is replaced at the War Station at home by its 1st Reserve unit'. The 2nd Reserve (later third-line) unit was to be raised at the depot or peace-time headquarters of the original unit and was to act as a training and draft-producing depot for both the first- and the second-line units. It was frequently referred to as the 'third-line depot', which led to confusion with the depots already constituted on mobilisation (see below). In present-day terminology 'training battalion' would be the most apt description of the third-line infantry unit.

The idea that second-line units would be relieved of responsibility for the provision of casualty replacement drafts for first-line units at the front and would be kept as fully trained units for the defence of the United Kingdom proved unworkable in practice, and drafts of men fit for foreign service were called for from both second- and third-line, as need arose. The difficulty of keeping up a steady supply of reinforcements for both first- and second-line battalions led in August 1916 to changes in the arrangements for training Territorial recruits, which reflected similar changes in the training of Regular recruits and led to the eventual removal of second-line Territorial battalions from Home Service divisions and their disbandment. They were replaced by Graduated Home Service battalions.

*Territorial Force Regulations* provided for Territorial Force Depots to be formed on mobilisation as directed by G.Os.C.-in-C. Their purpose was to attest, medically examine, clothe and equip recruits before despatching them for training (which, it was orginally envisaged, would take place with units at war stations but, from November 1914, took place in third-line units). The introduction of the term '3rd-Line Depot' in Army Council Instructions authorising the raising of third-line units led to some confusion as to the role of the existing depot and the new 'training' unit and clarifying instructions were issued in March 1915.[3] In April 1915 the titles of the original Territorial Force Depots were altered to 'Territorial Force Administrative Centres'. It had always been intended that where convenient Territorial Force Depots would cover more than one locally-raised unit and steps were taken as the war progressed to encourage, or insist upon, the amalgamation of depots originally raised for single units and the use of 'all arms county depots' wherever possible.[4] By the autumn of 1917 the purpose of Territorial Force Administrative Centres – they had in fact been redesignated 'Depots', in August 1916 – had all but lapsed and they were disbanded, their duties, in the case of infantry battalions, being taken over by Infantry Regimental Depots.

## 4.4   2nd/1st Battalion 1914-1917

Action was taken under A.C.I. 310 of August 1914 to raise 1st (Reserve) Battalion The Hertfordshire Regiment in September 1914 and Colonel Sir Charles Longmore, K.C.B., V.D. was appointed to command. The early organisation was in eight lettered companies but the areas from which they were raised did not all correspond to those of the 1st Battalion shown in Table 4.2. It is, in any case, very doubtful if the area assocations were maintained for long, and certainly not after the change to the four-company organisation under Army Order 54 of 1915, which took place in January 1915. Thereafter, until June 1915, A and B Companies consisted of Imperial Service men and C and D Companies of Home Service men. The original intention that the battalion, which was designated 2nd/1st Battalion at the end of January 1915, should replace the 1st/1st Battalion at its war station with 54th (East Anglian) Division was abandoned in April 1915 when the division was warned for service abroad with first-line units only. The gap in 162 (1st/1st East Midland) Infantry Brigade was filled by 1st/10th London Regiment and the 2nd/1st Battalion was then confirmed as part of 207 (2nd/1st East Midland) Infantry Brigade in 69th (2nd East Anglian) Division. The division was then stationed in the Peter-borough area but shortly moved to Suffolk, where the battalion was stationed at Newmarket. Home Service officers and men were posted from the battalion to 68th Provisional Battalion (later designated 11th Battalion The Bedfordshire Regiment) in June 1915 and for some time thereafter 2nd/1st Battalion, with a strength of nearly one thousand officers and men, was organised with two 'service' companies (A and B), consisting of trained men with a proportion of recruits over nineteen years of age, and two 'training' companies (C and D) consisting almost entirely of recruits. In November 1915 2nd/1st Battalion received orders to reduce its other rank strength to four hundred, against a new establishment of six hundred, by transfers to 3rd/1st Battalion. A few days later the battalion was split in two to form in addition the 4th/1st Battalion (see below). From its minimal strength of two hundred it was shortly brought back up to a strength of four hundred by drafts from 3rd/1st Battalion. Early in 1916 Home Service men were once again taken on strength and the battalion was again over one thousand all ranks when it moved with 69th Division to the Harrogate area of Yorkshire in June 1916. The battalion moved twice

Figure 4.11 *The Hertfordshire Regiment – Two privates, probably of the 2nd/1st Battalion, c. 1916. They are wearing the 1914 Pattern Leather Equipment and are holding 'long' Lee-Enfield rifles, not then in general use in operational theatres.*(Private collection)

while in Northern Command and was disbanded in September 1917 as part of the extensive remodelling of the infantry brigades of 69th Division under which second-line Territorial battalions were replaced by Graduated Home Service battalions.

### 4.5   3rd/1st Battalion 1915–1917

A '2nd Reserve' battalion was raised at Hertford in December 1914 under authority of A.C.I. 271 of November 1914 and Lieutenant-Colonel H. Baker, V.D., was appointed to command. The battalion was redesignated 3rd/1st Battalion in February 1915. During the summer of 1915 the battalion moved to Windsor where the 'Third-Line Group' of the 54th (East Anglian) Division was being assembled. By October 1915 the Group had moved to Halton Park near Tring, which became the permanent home of the training battalions associated with the division for the rest of the war. In April 1916 the battalion was redesignated 1st (Reserve) Battalion The Hertfordshire Regiment.[5] The battalion was retained as the Regimental Reserve of the Hertfordshire Regiment in the sweeping reform of recruit training instituted under A.C.I. 1528/1916 and taking effect on 1 September 1916, when the Third-Line Group was redesignated the East Anglian Reserve Brigade. News of further economies in the recruit training organisation and the probable amalgamation of the 1st Reserve Battalion The Hertfordshire Regiment with the 5th Reserve Battalion The Bedfordshire Regiment broke at least as early as mid-June 1917. Despite protests from the County, the battalion was absorbed into 5th Reserve Battalion The Bedfordshire   [67]

Regiment in August 1917 and its title was lost, although within the reconstituted 5th Battalion two 'wings', each of two companies and known as the Hertfordshire Wing and the Bedfordshire Wing, were maintained.

## 4.6   4th/1st Battalion 1915–1917

Orders to split 2nd/1st Battalion to form an additional second-line battalion were received in mid-November 1915 (see above) and 4th/1st Battalion was formed from a cadre of 200 other ranks supplied by 2nd/1st Battalion. Lieutenant-Colonel J.D. Hunt was appointed to command. The battalion replaced the disbanding 2nd/4th Battalion The Essex Regiment in 206 (2nd/1st Essex) Infantry Brigade of 69th (2nd East Anglian) Division at Thetford, Norfolk during December 1915. In June 1916 the brigade moved to Harrogate, Yorkshire, and in May 1917 moved again to Welbeck, Nottinghamshire. Demobilisation of 4th/1st Battalion was ordered in mid-July 1917 and the battalion was disbanded at the end of August, Lieutenant-Colonel Hunt having held command throughout.

## 4.7   Regimental Depot 1914–1917

A Regimental Depot (later Administrative Centre) for the Hertfordshire Regiment was formed at Hertford on mobilisation. In August 1916 it was incorporated into the All Arms Territorial Force Depot, Hertford, which served in addition the Hertfordshire Yeomanry and 4th East Anglian Brigade, Royal Field Artillery. The reception, clothing and equipping of recruits for the Hertfordshire Regiment was taken over by the Regimental Depot of The Bedfordshire Regiment at Kempston, Bedford during the summer of 1917, when the Hertfordshire Regiment component, in fact the last remaining, of the All Arms Depot at Hertford was disbanded.

As the only battalion to serve abroad, the 1st/1st Battalion was the sole claimant to battle honours for the First World War. Twenty-two were awarded to the regiment in a list published with Army Order 49 of March 1924. A further four had been added by the time the final list of the First World War battle honours was published with Army Order 55 in February 1925. The regiment's full list, with the ten honours selected to be borne on the King's Colour [6] shown in capital letters, is as follows:

> 'YPRES, 1914, '17', 'Nonne Bosschen', 'FESTUBERT, 1915', 'LOOS', 'SOMME, 1916, '18', 'Thiepval', 'Ancre Heights', 'ANCRE, 1916', 'PILCKEM', 'Menin Road', 'Polygon Wood', 'Broodseinde', 'Poelcappelle', 'Passchendaele', 'St. QUENTIN', 'Rosières', 'Lys', 'Kemmel', 'Albert, 1918', 'Bapaume, 1918', 'HINDENBURG LINE', 'Havrincourt', 'Cambrai, 1918', 'Selle', 'SAMBRE', 'FRANCE AND FLANDERS, 1914–18'.

The regiment's application for a further honour for 'Scherpenberg' – the last battle in the defence of Flanders against the German offensive in April 1918 – was turned down after prolonged argument, on the grounds that insufficient numbers of 1st/1st Battalion were present to justify award. The cost of these honours was high, for over nine hundred officers and men, all but a few of whom lost their lives with 1st/1st Battalion in France and Flanders, are commemorated on the regimental war memorial in All Saints'

Church, Hertford. No record of the number of wounded, seriously or otherwise, survives. In addition to the two Victoria Crosses mentioned above, over three hundred decorations and mentions-in-despatches were awarded to members of the 1st/1st Battalion and a further thirty to members of the second- and third-line units and to officers in 'extra-regimental' appointments.

NOTES

1. A.C.I. 310/August 1914

2. A.O. 399/1914; A.C.I.s 198/October 1914, 271/November 1914, 266/December 1914, 258/January 1915, 240/February 1915, 72 and 243/March 1915 and 146/April 1915

3. A.C.I. 72/March 1915

4. A.C.I.s 648 and 1496/1916

5. A.C.I. 768/1916

6. A.O.s. 338 and 470/1922

# Chapter 5

# *The Hertfordshire Regiment 1920–1961*

## 5.1  1st Battalion 1920–1939

Instructions for the re-formation of 1st Battalion The Hertfordshire Regiment were issued in February 1920. Regrettably, early correspondence included the unit under the Bedfordshire and Hertfordshire Regiment, Territorial Army, as the 6th Battalion. It is no longer possible to say whether this was a mistake or a real attempt, now that the title of the Bedfordshire Regiment had been altered to reflect its long-standing links with Hertfordshire, to remove the Hertfordshire Regiment from the *Army List*. Swift action to ward off the implied threat of absorption was taken in the County and the War Office confirmed that the reconstituted 1st Battalion would indeed be of the Hertfordshire Regiment. (The fact that the unit would have been senior to the existing Territorial battalion of the Bedfordshire and Hertfordshire Regiment and hence should properly have been the 5th Battalion does not seem to have been taken up.)

Under the command of Lieutenant-Colonel H. Page Croft, C.M.G., T.D. and with Colonel Sir Charles Longmore, K.C.B., V.D., T.D. as Honorary Colonel, the battalion was quickly up to its establishment of just over 650 all ranks, with a good proportion of both officers and men who had previously served with the Hertfordshire Regiment. By the end of 1921 headquarters and outlying detachments had been established as shown in Table 5.1.

It was some time before the complete order of battle of the new Territorial Army had been agreed and the battalion's title and its place in 162 (East Midland) Infantry Brigade of 54th (East Anglian) Division were not confirmed until December 1922.[1] Uniform and badges did not change from those worn prior to the First World War except that it was agreed in September 1920 that the battalion should wear a scarlet cloth 'ace of hearts' on the upper arm in khaki service dress. Full dress was almost entirely discontinued but may have been worn by officers attending levées.

Perhaps not surprisingly, given the financial stringency in defence matters in the 1920s and '30s, some smaller outlying detachments were closed at intervals and the drill stations at Baldock, Harpenden, Hatfield, Sawbridgeworth and Stevenage lost to the battalion. Major change in organisation was not to take place until 1938–39 but in 1929 it was announced that Territorial infantry battalions would reorganise on the basis of three rifle companies and one machine-gun company by April 1930. No. 3 Company accordingly absorbed the personnel of the machine-gun platoon, already located at Bishop's Stortford, and became the battalion machine-gun company. Also in 1930 the increasing number of personnel attached to battalion headquarters was recognised by the creation of 'Headquarters Wing', which was intially based with battalion headquarters in Hertford but gradually encroached on Ware, so much so that eventually the headquarters of No. 1 Company was moved to Watford

TABLE 5.1   *1st Battalion The Hertfordshire Regiment – 1921*

| | |
|---|---|
| Battalion Headquarters | Hertford |
| No. 1 Company<br>Detachments | Hertford<br>   St. Albans, Hatfield, Harpenden |
| No. 2 Company<br>Detachments | Hemel Hempstead<br>   Watford, Berkhamsted, Tring |
| No. 3 Company<br>Detachments | Bishop's Stortford<br>   Ware, Hoddesdon, Sawbridgeworth, Waltham Cross |
| No. 4 Company<br>Detachments | Hitchin<br>   Stevenage, Baldock, Letchworth |
| Machine-Gun Platoon | Bishop's Stortford |
| Corps of Drums | Ware |

and the Hertford–Ware area was devoted entirely to the provision of personnel for Headquarters Wing.

Lieutenant-Colonel Sir Henry Page Croft, Bt., C.M.G., M.P., who combined a distinguished parliamentary career with command of the battalion, retired in February 1924 and was succeeded by Lieutenant-Colonel E.C.M.Phillips, D.S.O., T.D., who had already held command on active service (see pages 59–60). Lieutenant-Colonel Phillips was promoted to a Territorial Army Colonel's appointment (in which he was later mobilised) in January 1931 and succeeded by Lieutenant-Colonel H. Pawle, O.B.E., who had recently retired from the Regular Army. He, in turn, relinquished command in January 1937, eventually to be promoted brigadier to command 161 Infantry Brigade, and handed over to Lieutenant-Colonel J.A. Longmore, M.B.E., son of Colonel Sir Charles Longmore, who was destined to give comparable distinguished service to the regiment. Sir Charles had died in 1930 after fifty-two years continuous association with the Hertfordshire Regiment and its immediate predecessors and was succeeded as Honorary Colonel by Brigadier-General The Viscount Hampden, K.C.B., C.M.G., now Lord Lieutenant of Hertfordshire and under whose command the 1st Battalion had sailed for France in 1914.

The 1st Battalion provided detachments to take part in the Coronation celebrations of Their Majesties King George VI and Queen Elizabeth in May 1937, the first occasion on which the new 'Coronation' uniform, which was to replace the scarlet walking-out dress, was worn. Queen Elizabeth, who was born at St. Paul's Walden and retained close family links with Hertfordshire and a great interest in the county, was, to the delight of all ranks, appointed Honorary Colonel of the 1st Battalion – the only battalion then existing – in February 1938. Her tenure of the appointment, during which she took a close personal interest in the regiment and was greatly respected and loved by all with whom she came into contact, ended after twenty-three years, when the regiment became unidentifiable after amalgamation. Her links with Hertfordshire's Territorial infantry were not entirely severed, however, as she became in turn Colonel-in-Chief of the 3rd East Anglian Regiment and the Royal Anglian Regiment.

The pace of life throughout the Territorial Army changed markedly during the summer and autumn of 1938. Re-equipment, and some consequent reorganisation, was in the air before the Munich crisis, which served to underline the urgency of these very necessary moves, designed in the case of the infantry to fit battalions for a more mobile role and to introduce a greater variety of supporting weapons. Territorial infantry battalions

Figure 5.1   *1st Battalion The Hertfordshire Regiment – H.R.H. The Prince of Wales inspects a guard of honour found by the battalion at St. Albans, 1924.*

(Regimental collection)

Figure 5.2   *1st Battalion The Hertfordshire Regiment – The officers of the battalion in service dress, 1932. Note that officers entitled to be mounted on parade and in the field – the C.O., Second-in-Command, Company Commanders and the Adjutant – are wearing breeches with field boots and spurs, while remaining officers are wearing 'plus four' style trousers.*

(Regimental collection)

Figure 5.3   *1st Battalion The Hertfordshire Regiment – Life in the battalion in the 1930s: Battalion shooting team c. 1934 (Top); Range-takers' test, mid-1930s (Centre); Field training dress (warm weather!) with respirators, probably 1938 (Bottom).*
(Hertford Museum – Top; Private collection – Centre and Bottom)

Figure 5.4  *1st Battalion The Hertfordshire Regiment – The Coronation Detachment in their new blue uniforms, 1937.*

(Regimental collection)

underwent comprehensive reorganisation in November 1938, when rifle companies were reduced from four platoons to three, 'headquarters wing' was finally recognised as a company and the battalion machine-gun company was abolished, medium machine-guns now being grouped in machine-gun battalions. As a result the 1st Battalion adopted new organisation and locations as shown in Table 5.2.

This organisation was short-lived and the battalion never put it into practice at annual camp, for in March 1939 instructions were received, as part of the nationwide increases in the Territorial Army, for the battalion to recruit beyond full war establishment and split in two to form an additional battalion. Success in recruiting was such that by the end of April, and before any other battalion outside London, Lieutenant-Colonel

TABLE 5.2  *1st Battalion The Hertfordshire Regiment – November 1938*

| | |
|---|---|
| Battalion Headquarters | Hertford |
| Headquarters Company | Hertford |
|   Signals, Carrier, Pioneer and | Hertford |
|   Administration Platoons | |
|   Mortar and A.-A. L.M.G. Platoons | Ware |
| No. 1 Company | St. Albans |
|   Detachment |   Watford |
| No. 2 Company | Hemel Hempstead |
|   Detachment |   Berkhamsted |
| No. 3 Company | Bishop's Stortford |
|   Detachments |   Hoddesdon, Waltham Cross, Widford |
| No. 4 Company | Hitchin |
|   Detachment |   Letchworth |
| Corps of Drums | Ware |

Figure 5.5 (On facing page)  *Brigadier J. A. Longmore, C.B., C.B.E., T.D. (1899–1973) First appointed to the 1st Battalion The Hertfordshire Regiment 1922; Commanding Officer, 1st Battalion 1936–41; Honorary Colonel 1952–62. He is wearing pre-1914 pattern full dress.*

Longmore was able to report that the required strength had been reached and that the split could proceed. Local enthusiasm was some way ahead of the authorities' capacity to implement the necessary administrative changes, however, and, as was the case with many units, the Hertfordshire Regiment went to annual camp in 1939 as a greatly over-strength 1st Battalion. Forty officers and over 1200 men attended, of whom about half had enlisted within the year since the previous camp. It had, meanwhile, been agreed that the new unit would be located in the south and west of the county, leaving the north and east to the 1st Battalion, and at a ceremonial parade at the end of camp Nos. 1 and 2 Companies were ordered to march off to form what was soon to be known as the 2nd Battalion.

The details of the reorganised units were finally approved in mid-August 1939, the 1st Battalion adopting the locations shown in Table 5.3 and it was with this organisation that the battalion mobilised under Lieutenant-Colonel Longmore's command as part of 162 Infantry Brigade (1st and 2nd Battalions The Hertfordshire Regiment and 6th Battalion The Bedfordshire and Hertfordshire Regiment) in 54th (East Anglian) Division on 1 September 1939.

TABLE 5.3   *1st Battalion The Hertfordshire Regiment – August 1939*

| | |
|---|---|
| Battalion Headquarters | Hertford |
| Headquarters Company | Hertford (less one platoon)<br>Ware (one platoon) |
| No. 1 Company | Bishop's Stortford (less one platoon)<br>Ware (one platoon) |
| No. 2 Company | Letchworth |
| No. 3 Company | Waltham Cross (less one platoon)<br>Hoddesdon (one platoon) |
| No. 4 Company | Hitchin (less one platoon)<br>Royston (one platoon) |

## 5.2   1st Battalion 1939–1946

The 1st Battalion followed the fortunes of its parent brigade – 162 Infantry Brigade – within 54th (East Anglian) Division for the first three years of the war, which were spent in the defence of the United Kingdom. During September 1939, after completion of mobilisation, the combined 1st/2nd Battalion remained in Hertfordshire, based on the peace-time drill halls, and continued training and finalising the arrangements for the split into two units, which took place on 1 October. At the end of October 54th Division deployed in a counter-invasion role on the East Anglian coast and the battalion occupied positions in the Harwich–Felixstowe area, where they were to remain for nearly six months. In April 1940 54th Division was moved to Northumberland where it continued in the coast defence role, initially under command of Northern Command and, from July 1940 following a re-arrangement of the Home Defence chain of command, under X Corps. The division was still short of vehicles, guns and infantry support weapons and, while a covering force was always dug in on the coast, much ingenuity had to be shown in defending large areas of the hinterland by 'flying columns' which would have been used either against parachute landings or in a divisional reserve or counter-attack role. Exceptionally hard weather during the winter of 1940–41 added to the battalion's difficulties. In March 1941 54th Division was placed in G.H.Q. reserve and concentrated in the area of Cheltenham, Gloucestershire. It was here, at the end of April 1941, that Lieutenant-Colonel J.A. Longmore, M.B.E., T.D. handed over command of the 1st Battalion to Lieutenant-Colonel A.C. Young, a Regular officer of the Bedfordshire and Hertfordshire Regiment. Colonel Longmore was posted to the War Office, where he served as Deputy Director, Territorial Army, Home Guard and Cadets until demobilisation.

Towards the end of July 1941 54th Division moved again, still in G.H.Q. reserve, to Buckinghamshire. Here, for the first time since mobilisation, the 1st Battalion was concentrated in one place – Dropmore Hall, Burnham – where they remained for four months. The division, by now visibly better equipped and trained, moved back to East Anglia and came under command of XI Corps in November 1941. The 1st Battalion occupied positions around Kessingland, immediately south of Lowestoft, Suffolk, for just over nine months.

Essential as their role had been in the ground defence of the United Kingdom, the 1st Battalion was relieved to be nominated for service abroad after three years of hard training during which the expected invasion had never materialised and the worst enemies had been the weather, boredom and the directing staff and umpires of numerous anti-invasion exercises. On 7 September 1942 they left 162 Infantry Brigade and moved to Brigg, Lincolnshire, to mobilise for overseas service.

The battalion was brought up to war establishment by drafts from various East Anglian units and speculation began on their eventual destination. India and North Africa attracted the shortest odds. Meanwhile changes were made in the organisation of the battalion, first to only three rifle companies and a support/administration company, then back to four rifle companies and 'headquarters' company. In mid-November Lieutenant-Colonel G.W.H. Peters, M.C., also a Regular Bedfordshire and Hertfordshire Regiment officer, arrived to take over from Lieutenant-Colonel Young. During March 1943 it was confirmed, to the general disappointment of all ranks, who had hoped the battalion would at last take part in active operations, that they were in fact to join the Fortress Garrison in Gibraltar. The advance party left by air on 31 March and the main body followed by sea, embarking at Glasgow on 13 April to arrive in Gibraltar on 22 April. The battalion shared a troopship with the 2nd Battalion The Royal Scots, alongside whom they were to work, and later fight, for more than two years.

Writing immediately after the war, a battalion correspondent to *The Wasp* admitted that while their fifteen months tour on the Rock may have been of importance to the war effort as a whole, it was 'far from what we had hoped'. Nevertheless, as part of 2 Gibraltar Brigade (April – November 1943) and then 1 Gibraltar Brigade (November 1943 – July 1944), the battalion cheerfully carried out all the duties of overseas garrison troops. These included guards on the naval base and dockyard, airfield, tunnel entrances and other vulnerable points and assistance at the customs posts on the frontier with Spain. The ceremonial aspect of guard duties continued, with the battalion taking its turn to find the Government House guard and regularly participating in the traditional 'Ceremony of the Keys'. In addition to these guard tasks the battalion was assigned a role in the defence of the Rock against large-scale attack and regularly practised the occupation of the fixed defences. Extension of the tunnel network inside

Figure 5.6    *1st Battalion The Hertfordshire Regiment – Expansion of the Territorial Army as seen at Watford, April 1939. (Top) A squad undergoing foot- and arms drill instruction. Note the lance-corporal in the new denim fatigue dress with khaki field service cap (centre foreground). (Centre) A class training on the Bren light machine-gun in the anti-aircraft role. (Bottom) A cheerful load in one of the battalion's new Guy 15 cwt trucks.*

(Watford Library)

Figure 5.7 *1st Battalion The Hertfordshire Regiment – Expansion of the Territorial Army, April 1939 (Top) The social side of the Territorial Army was not neglected – potential recruits at the dartboard at Watford. Note the corporal in 'blues'.*
(Watford Library)
*(Centre) A warrant officer demonstrating the .55-in. Boyes anti-tank rifle to admiring A.R.P. wardens at Letchworth. (Bottom) A team showing the newly-introduced Bren light machine-gun to a more sceptical crowd of youngsters.*
(Hitchin Museum)

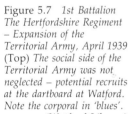

[79]

Figure 5.8   *The Hertfordshire Regiment – (Left top) – Other ranks' brass shoulder title adopted instead of that shown in Figure 4.2 during 1939. The authority for the removal of the 'T' is not recorded but the title was in widespread use in service dress, battledress and khaki drill until 1943, when it seems largely to have been replaced by the white-on-red cloth title shown below. (Actual size 52mm. × 10mm.) (Left centre) Embroidered slip-on shoulder title (black letters on khaki) worn in battle dress 1939 – 1943 (Actual size 72 mm. × 41 mm.) (Left bottom) Shoulder title (white letters on scarlet) worn in battle dress 1943 – 1961). (Width 116 mm.)*          (J. D. Sainsbury)
*(Centre)    1st Battalion The Hertfordshire Regiment – Other ranks' khaki service dress, complete with collar badges and brass shoulder titles, as worn with the khaki field service cap for several months after mobilisation, in this case in February 1940. (Right) Battledress, 1937 Pattern, as issued to the battalion in the spring of 1940. The 54th Division flash can be distinguished above the drummer's badge.*          (H. G. Pasfield)

[80]   Figure 5.9   *1st Battalion The Hertfordshire Regiment – The Corps of Drums, in battledress with pre-war service dress caps, on parade in Cheltenham, March 1941.*          (H. G. Pasfield)

the Rock took place throughout the war and all garrison units, including the 1st Battalion, provided working parties to assist the Royal Engineers in digging and maintaining the tunnels and chambers and to move stores and supplies. Training facilities on the Rock were limited and it was important to make the best possible use of them. This the battalion did, holding route marches 'up, round, over and down the Rock', which helped maintain a high level of fitness and provided a familiarity with mountainous terrain which was to prove very useful when they went into action later. A training camp was established near Oran on the North African mainland and companies were able to pass through the camp and take part in more mobile exercises and field firing. Very good use was made of the considerable opportunity for all kinds of sport as a means of maintaining both fitness and morale. The Regimental Band arrived in Gibraltar shortly after the main body and from then on was fully engaged. Not only did it take part in the many military parades and occasions, but it gave regular concerts and provided the dance band at the Rock Hotel.

Eventually, after this period of 'drudgery, disillusion, boredom and frustration', as Colonel Peters later described it, arrangements were made for relief of the battalion by a garrison battalion, 30th Battalion The Dorset Regiment, and in July 1944 it was at last ordered to move into an operational theatre – Italy – where the Allied advance had reached the River Arno. With a total strength of just over nine hundred all ranks and organised with Battalion Headquarters, Headquarters Company, Support Company, four rifle companies (Nos. 1–4) and a 'details' company holding first-line reinforcements and others 'left out of battle' and known as No.

*Figure 5.10  1st Battalion The Hertfordshire Regiment – The Drums, now in khaki drill with shorts, lead the guard, just visible behind, and wearing topees, on to guard mounting parade at Government House, Gibraltar, June 1943. The Drums accompanied the battalion to Italy, where they served in the anti-tank platoon and as stretcher bearers.*　　　　　　　(H. G. Pasfield)

5 Company, the battalion embarked in two small ships on 22 July 1944. To their regret it was not possible to organise a ceremonial march past the Governor and companies moved independently to the docks with the band doing its best to get round to each in turn. No. 1 Company were at Gibraltar Training Camp in North Africa and they embarked separately without returning to the Rock and sailed for Italy in an American troopship to meet the main body of the battalion on arrival. This early introduction to the United States Army, with which the battalion was to come into frequent contact later, was fortuitous. As the two ships carrying the battalion left the quayside the regimental band, which was due to remain in Gibraltar, played regimental music but it was a somewhat false farewell, for the ships then remained for three days within the confines of the harbour. When they finally moved it was, evidently for security reasons, westwards into the Atlantic, where they joined a much larger convoy to sail back past Gibraltar on the morning of the 26th. The battalion landed at Naples on 29 July and marched to a transit camp on the outskirts of the city. Here, in unpleasant conditions and pestered by the local popu-lation, many of whom were starving, they remained for five days, drawing full war establishment of vehicles, heavy weapons and other equipment. By the evening of 3 August they were ready, and indeed anxious, to move out of the Naples area.

On 4 August 1st Battalion The Hertfordshire Regiment came under command of 66 Infantry Brigade. This newly formed brigade consisted of battalions recently released from garrison duty in the Mediterranean, the other two battalions being 2nd Battalion The Royal Scots, also from Gibraltar, and 11th Battalion The Lancashire Fusiliers, from Malta. It had been planned that 66 Brigade would become the infantry brigade of 1st Armoured Division and the battalion moved to a training camp some twenty miles east of Cassino, where the division was concentrating for training and highly necessary 'work-up' exercises in infantry/armour co-operation and tactics. The plan was changed, however, and as part of the measures taken to fill the gaps in the Allied line caused by the departure

Figure 5.11   *1st Battalion The Hertfordshire Regiment – A sergeant of the battalion on a course at Gibraltar Training Camp in North Africa, October 1943.*
(© Imperial War Museum)

of United States formations for the landings in Southern France, 66 Brigade was transferred to 1st Infantry Division and ordered to move to a concentration area immediately south of Florence – a convoy drive of some 220 miles which, in conditions of considerable difficulty, took three days. On arrival the battalion received orders to prepare to take over a sector of the front line astride the River Arno in Florence from a battalion of 8th Indian Division.

During the night of 21–22 August the battalion moved into Florence and deployed with three rifle companies across the river and one in reserve on the south side. The river, some two hundred yards wide, had to be crossed on the top of a weir by troops on foot and the battalion's wheeled vehicles, the carriers making a considerable detour to cross on a bailey bridge. The takeover was made more difficult by the fact that junior officers of the Indian battalion could not speak much English but soon after midnight the battalion was, at last, 'in the line'. Their positions were overlooked by the enemy, who occupied higher ground between eight hundred yards and one mile away and the battalion at once began energetic patrolling as a means of 'feeling' their way forward into the hills and dominating as much as possible of the ground in front of them. As a result of the information gained it proved possible to push the battalion's forward position about one thousand yards closer to the enemy and make preparations for an assault on a local strongpoint, the centuries-old castle at Vincigliato.

An attempt by No. 2 Company to take the castle by stealth in daylight on 25 August failed and the company withdrew, suffering the battalion's first casualties in action from enemy mortar defensive fire. By 28 August all the forward companies had established themselves in the foothills and were patrolling aggressively. The battalion gained considerable ground between 31 August and 2 September, by-passing Vincigliato, which the enemy abandoned shortly afterwards, and pressing on to the dominant high ground, Monte Cicere. This position fell to a frontal assault over very steep and difficult ground by No. 4 Company while No. 2 Company outflanked the heights and took the enemy by surprise from the rear. Enemy resistance was poor, and sensing the opportunity of gaining further ground the two leading companies (Nos. 1 and 2) succeeded in outflanking Fiesole, an important junction, and capturing it after about an hour's brisk fighting. On 2 September the battalion was ordered to push on north from Fiesole towards Borgo San Lorenzo to clear the main axis of advance. Leaving No. 4 Company on Monte Cicere to cover their subsequent movements, the battalion withdrew into the suburbs of Florence and emerged on the main axis, a little to the east of their original advance.

A co-ordinated push by Nos. 2 and 4 Companies cleared the main axis for some four miles, after which the forward elements found themselves isolated at the point of a salient (for neighbouring units had not made similar progress) and out of range of the battalion's mortars and supporting artillery. After nightfall the forward companies were repositioned and reserves brought up and the carriers and mortars pushed forward to give much needed fire support. Thus reorganised, the battalion, and notably No. 3 Company, were able to beat off a determined counter-attack that began in bright moonlight and lasted until shortly after dawn on 3 September. There was no further advance before the battalion was relieved on the night of 4–5 September. No. 1 Company, attempting a daylight occupation of advanced positions on 4 September were caught by mortar fire before they had had chance to dig in properly, and were forced to withdraw with casualties. The two forward companies, Nos. 3 and 4, patrolled extensively during the two days and provided vauable information on the enemy's locations and movements. It became clear that his overall plan was to withdraw to the safety (albeit temporary) of his previously prepared 'Gothic Line', just to the north.

On 12 September the battalion moved back into the forward positions, as left flank unit of 1st Infantry Division with United States troops on their immediate left. The terrain was now mountainous, as opposed to hilly, which it had been a little further south, and the battalion first took up a position with two companies on a wooded forward slope facing, across a precipitous, rocky valley, the enemy's Gothic Line, at least two thousand feet from the valley bottom and towering over the battalion positions. The enemy was determined and in well prepared positions with wire and other obstacles and expertly placed defensive fire. Within the next few days the 1st Battalion, in a renowned feat of arms, were to attack these positions in daylight and seize them, together with about fifty prisoners, for minimal casualties.

The assault on the Gothic Line was due to take place on 14 September, so there was very little time, once the battalion was back in the line, for reconnaissance and preparation. They spent the 13th filtering forward until by evening they were well established on a wooded hill looking across a valley at the enemy and had secured a most valuable asset – a close and well covered start line for the attack. It was believed that the enemy had, at most, very little idea of the significance of any movement he did detect on the battalion's frontage.

The attack was so timed as to allow the greater part of the day for softening up the enemy positions. Shelling, by the divisional artillery's four regiments and an additional heavy regiment, began at 09.00 and continued until H-hour at 16.30, giving just enough time for the attackers to fight their way on to their objectives in daylight. The advance was on a one-company frontage, with No. 3 Company leading on to the first known enemy positions and No. 2 Company passing through to the battalion objective, which was short of the actual summit. The Lancashire Fusiliers would then move forward to seize the highest point, Poggio Prefetto.

Under cover of smoke, which was laid both to blind and deceive the enemy, the leading company got down to and across the valley unseen and at a place which was judged such an unlikely crossing point that it would not be covered by enemy defensive fire. They quickly manoeuvred behind the enemy's outposts before he had even realised that the attack had started. Surprise and the day's shelling assured a quick collapse and surrender. Resistance on the long climb was confined to sniping and occasional machine-gun fire. The real difficulty was the mountain itself, which was in places unclimbable. The heavy weight of ammunition, radios, cable and tools that had to be carried added to the task. Nevertheless, as the commanding officer later recorded, 'Good junior leadership, combined with the exhilaration of early successes, enabled Nos. 2 and 3 Companies, which had become rather intermixed, to reach the top of the mountain by 18.05 – half an hour earlier than had been thought possible'.

In gathering darkness the two assault companies organised themselves to defend the newly won position against the expected counter-attack which, to their surprise, did not materialise. Meanwhile No. 1 Company struggled up by another route to reinforce the position around the crest and a mule track was reconnoitred to enable the forward companies to be resupplied and fed early the next morning. Patrols were sent out almost at once and a feeble counter-attack was repulsed by United States units advancing on the left to seize a neighbouring crest. The American attack was successful and a further commanding feature fell to their advance shortly afterwards. The first break in the Gothic Line had been well and truly made, with the battalion playing a crucial part in the action.

On 20 September the battalion resumed the advance, setting out to outflank the enemy on his right and secure two features – Poggio del'Altello and Monte Carzolano – overlooking the next valley. A force consisting of No. 1 Company in the lead, followed by a reduced Battalion Headquarters and then Nos. 4 and 2 Companies set out in single file through thick woods in heavy rain and low cloud, which further concealed their movements from the enemy. Mortars and machine-guns were left behind but reserve ammunition accompanied the column on mule back, as did an artillery forward observation party. By midday, after some three hours steady progress, the force had advanced out of range of its supporting artillery and reached more open country where they were held up by a precipitous ravine. Reconnaisance of a route across and further probing forward took until 16.30 at which point the mist came right down and the bulk of the force were able to cross, finding to their dismay that the climb out on the northern side was too difficult for the mules. In gathering dusk and atrocious weather No. 2 company secured the bridgehead while Nos.1 and 4 Companies attempted to push on. Shortly afterwards, with only a few minutes of daylight left, the leading platoon of No. 1 Company spotted a party of some forty enemy who were evidently oblivious of the presence of British troops. The subsequent fire fight lasted half an hour, during which the two leading companies succeeded in working round both flanks of the enemy, with the result that very few escaped. It was now dark; the battalion admitted to not knowing exactly where they were in very difficult country and they were out of touch with food, tools and heavy weapons. In a poor position to withstand any counter-attacks, which fortunately did not come, platoons stayed where they were, awaiting daylight and hoping that the mules with ammunition and food would somehow catch up with them.

As the mist cleared on the morning of 21 September it was realised that the left leading company was actually in possession of Poggio del'Altello and the right company well up the shoulder of Monte Carzolano, which was evidently clear of the enemy. They pushed on the remaining few hundred yards to the crest and there, to their astonishment, they found the Adjutant, R.S.M. and mule train, who, having failed to find the battalion, had positioned themselves on a dominant feature. 'It was good fortune rather than good map reading', the commanding officer later observed, 'which brought us out on the right objective'. But the success was real, for all that, and the brigade quickly followed up to consolidate the gain, which was considerable. For the first time they were on higher ground than the enemy and with excellent visibility both to the flanks and for some six miles forward.

A change in the weather on the morning of 22 September, which dawned brilliantly fine, enabled the divisional artillery to engage targets as far forward as the small town of Paluzzuolo, the enemy's main headquarters and communications centre, and to cover fighting patrols sent out by the battalion, who were constantly trying to gain further ground.

Reviewing the first few days of operations against the Gothic Line, 1st Infantry Division's historian wrote,

> It is hard, on paper without the ground to look at, to convey an adequate impression of the seven days from 14th to 20th September 1944. To get an adequate picture it is necessary first to look from Borgo at the wall of mountains in front, then to climb Prefetto, and to climb down into and up the other side of some of the valleys which the troops crossed. Better still, try to climb some of the hills in rain and mist, with visibility only a few yards. It takes a strong and fit man, even with no enemy present . . .

The Battles Nomenclature Committee later recognised the period 25 August – 22 September as the period qualifying for the battle honour 'Gothic Line'. No honour was more deservedly awarded to the Hertfordshire Regiment, whose 1st Battalion had played such a vital role in penetrating the line on the 1st Infantry Division front. Regrettably, no subsidiary honour was available to recognise their signal contribution to the original break-in on 14 September.

The battalion finished their present tour in the line on 30 September. The intervening days were devoted to an operation to outflank and clear the enemy from Monte Gamberaldi, a position which was holding up the advance of a neighbouring brigade.

On 22 September two companies exploited north-east from Poggio del'Altello against little opposition, enabling the whole battalion to be concentrated on 23 September in a position immediately south-west of the key road junction, the small town of Palazzuolo. They occupied the town on 25 September and immediately pushed two companies through and on to higher ground beyond. From here a splendid night advance led by No. 1 Company resulted in the important Point 785 falling to the battalion early in the morning of 27 September. Later in the day Nos. 3 and 4 Companies occupied the associated Monte Toncone, with the result that the battalion were now in an excellent position to attack the obstinate Monte Gamberaldi from the north.

A reconnaissance was carried out at once. Faced with a night attack on a bare hill which dominated the start line by some five hundred feet and entailed an advance through sticky clay in very poor weather, the commanding officer recommended that the attack be postponed. He was overruled and the battalion mortars were ordered to register before dark targets in support of an attack to be led by No. 4 Company. In fact heavy mortar concentrations, rather than mere registering, were put down on the objective and the enemy's approaches from the rear. This heavy fire, together with the now evident threat from the flank, persuaded the enemy to withdraw at dusk, to the great relief of all, and the battalion was ordered to turn north again in pursuit.

It was important to keep up the momentum of the advance and during the 28th No. 3 Company struggled gallantly forward in very difficult weather conditions. They dislodged the enemy from one further important position by the now normal outflanking tactics and finally confronted him holding a strong position on a feature known as Point 714. No. 3 Company were ordered to contain the enemy on Point 714 while the Royal Scots worked round to the right. Some excellent patrol work by No. 3 Company, which lasted until after nightfall on 29 September, led to the attainment of the brigade objective. Meanwhile, the battalion, with the exception of No. 3 Company, was relieved and withdrawn on the night of 29–30 September. No. 3 Company, withdrawn from their exposed forward positions during darkness, had a very difficult journey down on the

Figure 5.12  *Brigadier G. W. H. Peters, C.B.E., D.S.O., M.C. – Commanding Officer, 1st Battalion The Hertfordshire Regiment November 1942 – September 1945; Honorary Colonel 1st Battalion The Bedfordshire and Hertfordshire Regiment 1962–67.*

morning of 30 September, carrying their wounded on mule back. The mules were as exhausted as the men and the stretchers had frequently to be taken off and carried over the worst going. Nevertheless they rejoined the battalion during the 30th and all ranks looked forward to a very well earned rest.

The battalion had been in the line for eighteen days, during which the advance had been almost continuous. As has already been mentioned, they frequently had to operate outside supporting artillery range and the battalion's own heavy weapons could only be brought into action with great difficulty and with limited ammunition stocks. But the overwhelming difficulty was that of routine resupply over incredibly difficult country. The carrier and anti-tank platoons, which could not in any case operate in the prevailing conditions, were re-formed into supply parties, working with both jeeps and mules but often having to rely on manpack in the steepest and most difficult areas. The sterling efforts of these parties are fully recorded in the *Hertfordshire Field Gazette* – a fitting and well-deserved tribute from their comrades.

Once out of the line early in October the battalion, in common with all British infantry battalions in Italy, was ordered to reduce from four rifle companies to three. No. 4 Company was accordingly disbanded and the personnel absorbed into other companies.

There was an extreme manpower shortage and such reinforcements as were reaching the battalion were largely from disbanding anti-aircraft artillery regiments and required both retraining and experience before they

[87]

became useful members of rifle platoons. (The former Royal Artillery personnel can be identified in battalion records and, for example, the roll of honour, from their army numbers in the 14000000 series. Original members of the battalion and reinforcements received through the East Anglian Infantry Depots have seven-figure numbers, the majority in the Bedfordshire and Hertfordshire Regiment series beginning 5950000 and 5960000.)

The battalion reoccupied front-line positions north-east of Palazzuolo on the night of 10–11 October, moving up through harassing fire over very difficult ground with casualties to both men and mules. As dawn broke on 11 October it became clear that the battalion's positions were dominated from the right by a feature called Monte Ceco, only part of which was in our hands. No. 2 Company were assigned an immediate counter-attack role in the event of the enemy regaining any further ground on Monte Ceco, leaving the battalion frontage to be held by Nos. 1 and 3 Companies. As the reduction in companies was not matched by a reduction in the frontage to be held, troops were 'thin on the ground' and it proved necessary to withdraw the carrier platoon from work on the supply routes and allocate a sector to them, with consequent increased difficulty in keeping the forward positions supplied with food and ammunition.

In preparation for an attack to clear the enemy from Monte Ceco it was necessary to secure Banzuole Ridge, a feature on the left of the frontage which overlooked Battalion Headquarters and the supply routes. No. 1 Company was given this task, and was allowed twenty-four hours for patrolling, reconnaissance and other preparations before attacking on the night of 11–12 October. The only method of approach turned out to be in single file and the company got to within one hundred yards without being detected. They still could not deploy, however, and were held up by machine-gun fire to their front and artillery defensive fire behind. The problem was solved by an artillery concentration on the enemy immediately in front – no mean feat on the Gunners' part in the dark and without accurate knowledge of our own troops' positions – after which it proved possible to rush the nearest post and deploy off the single track.

This little attack was very far from a text-book affair, but fortunately highly successful none the less, and it broke the stalemate and cleared the way for the advance over Monte Ceco, which was finally taken by the Lancashire Fusiliers after a fierce fight during the night of 16–17 October. The battalion then took over the Monte Ceco positions and established observation posts from which artillery and mortar fire were directed on to the enemy for the next two days. From the mountain it was possible to see the plains of Northern Italy opening out some eight to ten miles away.

The next few days, of large-scale patrol activity in an effort to find ways of continuing the advance, proved extremely difficult for the battalion and especially for No. 3 Company. A platoon from the company was ordered to capture Point 677, on a narrow ridge running north-east from the summit of Monte Ceco and to the battalion's front. Moving forward at dusk and in appalling weather the platoon surprised and over-ran the enemy post on the night of 18–19 October. They could not immediately be reinforced and were isolated and under attack, especially from enemy mortars, throughout the daylight hours of 19 October. At dusk a relieving party under O.C. No. 3 Company set out. It was heavily shelled almost immediately, the company commander was wounded and stores and equipment scattered. Under cover of the same shelling the enemy recaptured Point 677 and when the remnants of the company, most gallantly led by their wounded O.C., finally got within shouting distance it was clear that nothing would be achieved by attempting to press further forward. Casualties to the detached platoon and to the relieving force, especially in 'missing', were heavy. To make matters worse the company commander, who, despite being wounded a second time had controlled the withdrawal and evacuated the wounded, was killed, together with a number of other casualties, when harassing fire hit the Regimental Aid Post.

The combination of losses was such that the company had to be withdrawn from the line to absorb reinforcements, reorganise and train under new leaders. The remainder of the battalion stayed a further week on and around Monte Ceco in conditions of incessant rain and cold worse than any they had yet experienced in Italy and which tested the supply parties and mules to the limit of their endurance. Eventually the enemy gave way to pressure on his flanks and withdrew from Point 677, which the battalion occupied on 25 October. On the night of 26–27 October they withdrew to reserve positions, exhausted after a very arduous fortnight in the line.

On 7 November the battalion went forward once more, but this time to a change of scenery, for 1st Infantry Division had been switched to a new sector and had taken over from 88th U.S. Infantry Division in the hills to the south of Bologna. From the positions which the battalion took over on Monte Cerere the city could be clearly seen some eight miles away. The battalion's task was essentially defensive and they were opposed by an active and resolute enemy, the German 1st Parachute Division. The Americans had not been long in the area and there was much to be done to improve the defences. By the time the battalion first moved out to the rest area on the night of 23–24 November they had achieved a great deal in conditions of some difficulty, with snow, cold winds and several degrees of frost at night. As usual, everything had to be carried forward by man or mule under cover of darkness and every man of the battalion was roped in to assist – even the postal orderlies and clerks from Battalion Headquarters did their bit. As a result the defensive position was greatly improved, first by pushing further down the northern slopes to achieve greater depth, then by the provision of deep dug-outs and by the usual integrated fire plan of company and supporting weapons. The battalion themselves did not put their work to the test of a full scale enemy attack, which occurred shortly after their relief. To their satisfaction they heard that it had been repulsed with heavy casualties to the enemy who were reported to have been considerably surprised by the strength and depth of the positions and by the amount of wire.

On the night of 28–29 November the battalion returned to the divisional area, initially as divisional reserve. Meanwhile, the enemy had succeeded in regaining Monte Castellaro, a complementary feature to Monte Cerere on the left of the divisional sector, and preparations for a counter-attack by another unit were well advanced. The battalion spent the next two days in support of this counter-attack, which was not entirely successful, and then took over positions on and around Monte Castellaro, which they occupied until relieved on the night of 8–9 December. Enemy mortars, which were particularly active on the approaches to the battalion positions from the rear, gave everyone an uncomfortable time and made resupply difficult yet again. It seemed, also, that a period of winter stalemate was setting in, with neither side having quite the resources, now the campaign in North-West Europe was in full swing, to make real progress.

The battalion's return to the forward area on 15 December coincided with the onset of the mountain winter. Considerable resources and ingenuity had to be devoted to, at best, keeping warm or, at worst, preventing men, animals and weapons from freezing. Winter clothing was issued, including white camouflage suits, for there was now thick snow, and automatic weapons and mortars had to be fired at intervals to prevent them seizing up completely. Christmas Day was spent in the line without celebration; it proved impossible even to bring up much in the way of extra rations and festivities had to be postponed. The commanding officer later recorded, 'Nevertheless morale was excellent. The purity of the air and the beauty of the landscape acted as fine tonics for the spirit'. The contemporary *Hertfordshire Field Gazette* is cheerful but not nearly so poetic. However, a complete change of scene and weather was at hand, for the next period in the line, which lasted until 7 January and was uneventful except for the usual patrolling, turned out to be the last. The division had been ordered to the Eastern Mediterranean.

The 1st Battalion moved to Taranto by easy stages, arriving on 20 January 1945 and embarked with the rest of 66 Infantry Brigade on 27 January. On 31 January they disembarked at Haifa, in Palestine, and moved at once into a brigade concentration area at Pardes Hanna for a much needed period of rest, refitting and training. On 30 April 1945 the whole brigade moved into Syria for training and it was at Insiriya, just south of Beirut, that the battalion celebrated 'V.E.' Day, with two days holiday. Training in infantry/armour co-operation was carried out at Jebel Mazar, west of Damascus, during the second half of May and the brigade then returned to Camp 87 at Pardes Hanna. By this time quite a number of the longer-serving members of the battalion were leaving on various forms of release or prolonged leave and the battalion was considerably reorganised to take account of the large numbers coming in, both from training depots and from other units. The accent initially was on training, with three companies devoted to various forms of military training and pre-release education. Only Support Company and No. 3 (Duty) Company retained their orthodox roles under the reorganisation, though this was to change as the year progressed and operational demands increased. During July 1945 No. 3 Company provided guards on the Haifa oil pipeline for two weeks – a useful taste of things to come, though uneventful. Lieutenant-Colonel G.W.H. Peters, D.S.O., M.C. left the battalion at the end of September and for nearly two months, which included the battalion's first internal security operations, Major A. Andrews, D.S.O. acted as commanding officer until relieved by Lieutenant-Colonel H.C.R. Hose, D.S.O. towards the end of November.

Early in October 1945, while No. 1 Company and Support Company were detached to provide a fire-power demonstration for the Haifa Staff College, the rest of the battalion began making preparations to move from Camp 87 into winter quarters at Camp 520, ten miles north of Gaza. It was planned that the whole battalion would spend the second half of October making the camp habitable but the internal security situation was clearly deteriorating and between 10 and 20 October the commanding officer was ordered to 'recce' and plan for five different internal security tasks. On 20 October the battalion received orders to move to internal security tasks in the Tiberias area, which they did on 21 October, leaving only a rear party in Camp 520 and recalling Support Company, who were detached on exercise. The battalion formed part of a force commanded by C.R.A. 1st Infantry Division and known as 'Jordanforce'. The force, which consisted of two major units and a small number of minor units, was split into two groups, one at Rosh Pinna (1st King's Dragoon Guards less one squadron; No. 1 Company, 1st Battalion The Hertfordshire Regiment) and one at Tiberias (1st Battalion The Hertfordshire Regiment less one company; one squadron 1st K.D.G.). Force Headquarters was at Safad. The orders given to Jordanforce were 'to be prepared to keep communications open and to take offensive action as required'. Until the end of October this was interpreted as 'showing the flag' round the Jewish and Arab villages and settlements in each area and joint infantry/armour patrols went out each day with the additional purpose of getting to know the routes, possible ambush sites and vulnerable points throughout the area.

On the night of 31 October–1 November there was an outbreak of widespread sabotage throughout Palestine, directed at the railway network. Internal security measures were stepped up and extensive measures taken to check movement at night. The battalion took part in the introduction of these measures and was then withdrawn to Divisional Reserve at Camp 87 on 3 November. On 12 November the battalion deployed to guard the main railway line from Lydda to Hadera and, while on this duty, heard that they were to be transferred from 1st Infantry Division to 6th Airborne Division (without undertaking the airborne role or changing their headgear to maroon berets) on 18 November.

'I.S.' – Internal security – duties with 6th Airborne Division ground on for almost a year, with the additional complication of constant changes in personnel as more and more Territorials returned home for demobilisation. In January 1946 the battalion's base camp was moved back to Sarafand, where it remained until final dispersal. Companies went out on periods of operational duty in the surrounding area and returned for rest and training. The height of anti-terrorist activity was reached, as far as the battalion was concerned, in July and early August 1946. No. 3 Company took part in the rescue and clearance operations after the bomb outrage at the King David Hotel in Jerusalem in July. Shortly afterwards 2 Parachute Brigade Group, including 1st Battalion The Hertfordshire Regiment, was tasked with an immense 'cordon and search' operation, said to have been the largest operation of its kind that took place in Palestine, covering the whole of the city of Tel Aviv. Operation 'Shark', as it was known, took four days – 30 July to 2 August – during which many suspects were detained and some large dumps of arms and ammunition were found. Service in Palestine qualified members of the battalion for the award of the General Service Medal with Clasp 'Palestine 1945–48'.

On 1 November 1946 the battalion moved to Cairo in anticipation of the order for demobilisation. 'Suspended animation' took effect on 23 November, when some five hundred officers and men were drafted to Regular infantry battalions, including two hundred to 2nd Battalion The Bedfordshire and Hertfordshire Regiment. A representative cadre of thirty brought the battalion records (including the invaluable 'Overseas Service Diary' – an unofficial war diary) back to the Depot of the Bedfordshire and Hertfordshire Regiment at Kempston Barracks, Bedford, an event that passed without notice in Hertfordshire. However, as will be seen later, plans to restore the battalion to the post-war Territorial Army after its distinguished period of active service, were well in hand.

### 5.3   2nd Battalion 1939–1944

Instructions for the raising of a 'duplicate' unit of the Hertfordshire

Figure 5.13 *1st Battalion The Hertfordshire Regiment – A party from the battalion (in long trousers) working with Royal Engineers (in shorts) to recover bodies after the terrorist bomb attack on the King David Hotel, Jerusalem, July 1946.*

(G. H. Walker)

Figure 5.14 *1st Battalion The Hertfordshire Regiment – (Left) Firing party 'rest on arms reversed' at one of the funerals for victims of the King David Hotel outrage, Ramleh Commonwealth War Cemetery, Palestine, July 1946. (Right) A group of drivers in relaxed mood in front of a 6-pdr portee vehicle of the anti-tank platoon. Note especially the hart lodged vehicle sign (white on red) and that campaign medal ribbons are being worn, Sarafand, Palestine, 1946.*

(G. H. Walker)

Regiment were issued by War Office Letter dated 31 March 1939. As recorded above, the split into two separate units was not made until some months later. The initial idea that headquarters of the new battalion would be at Hemel Hempstead was overruled by the War Office on the grounds that too much new building would be required and in mid-August 1939 sub-unit locations were announced as shown in Table 5.4.

The battalion was not fully constituted, under the command of Lieutenant-Colonel Sir Giles Sebright, Bt., until 1 October 1939, having spent the first month of the war energetically preparing for the split while remaining

TABLE 5.4   *2nd Battalion The Hertfordshire Regiment – August 1939*

| | |
|---|---|
| Battalion Headquarters | Watford |
| Headquarters Company | Watford (less one platoon) Rickmansworth (one platoon) |
| No. 1 Company | St. Albans |
| No. 2 Company | Hemel Hempstead |
| No. 3 Company | Berkhamsted |
| No. 4 Company | Berkhamsted (less two platoons) Tring (two platoons) |

part of the 1st Battalion. Approval of the duplicate unit's title as '2nd Battalion The Hertfordshire Regiment' was published in A.C.I. 639/1939.

From October 1939 to mid-September 1942 the 2nd Battalion formed part of 162 Infantry Brigade in 54th (East Anglian) Division (see above). It deployed initially to counter-invasion positions in the Ipswich area, then moved to the Northumberland coast and between October 1940 and March 1941 was billeted near Morpeth, Northumberland. Both battalions were in the Cheltenham district from March to July 1941 and when the brigade moved to Buckinghamshire in July 1941 the 2nd Battalion was located in the area of Thame. On returning to the East Coast in November 1941 the battalion deployed around Southwold and later Woodbridge, in Suffolk, where they remained until transferred to 73 Independent Infantry Brigade in September 1942. The interlude with an independent brigade, which was spent in Cornwall, proved brief, for in December 1942 the 2nd Battalion returned to 54th (East Anglian) Division, but this time to 198 Infantry Brigade. (This brigade was not, in fact, East Anglian in origin, having joined the division in December 1940. It had been formed as a duplicate West Lancashire brigade and the other two battalions were 8th Battalion The King's Regiment and 6th Battalion The Border Regiment.) The division was still in East Anglia and the 2nd Battalion was deployed in the Ipswich area.

During the summer of 1943 54th Division was broken up and most of the constituent headquarters and units were retrained and assigned tasks in support of the forthcoming invasion of the continent of Europe (Operation 'Overlord'). In August Headquarters 198 Infantry Brigade became Headquarters 11 Lines of Communication Area and the three battalions, without losing their identities, were re-roled as the core units around which 'beach groups' were to be assembled. (A beach group was a mixed force which, in addition to the infantry battalion, comprised engineer, medical, supply and provost units, and at the height of its activity reached the size of an infantry brigade. The group landed with the assault units on a brigade front and took over from them the newly captured beachhead, running the first stores dumps to be established and thereafter assisting in the landing of troops, vehicles and stores across the beach and evacuating the wounded until eventually relieved by the full-scale lines of communication system.) For Operation Overlord six beach groups, paired to form three beach sub-areas, were allocated to the three beaches 'Gold', 'Juno' and 'Sword'.

The 2nd Battalion The Hertfordshire Regiment was the core battalion for No. 9 Beach Group. Training for their new role began in July 1943, when the battalion first took part in assault landing exercises on the East Coast and all officers went on a 'beach maintenance' course at one of the Combined Operations schools. In August the battalion moved to Scotland for three months' training at the Combined Operations Training Centre, during which the various other sub-units comprising No. 9 Beach Group were brought together under command of Lieutenant-Colonel J.R. Harper, commanding officer of the 2nd Battalion. Full-scale invasion exercises took place between the end of 1943 and April 1944, as a result of which the organisation of the beach group into landing-craft loads was perfected, as were the plan for their arrival on the beach in proper sequence and, of course, the vital movements and stores handling tasks with which they were entrusted. During May 1944 all troops taking part in the assault phases of Operation Overlord were, for security purposes, isolated in camps – in the 2nd Battalion's case in the New Forest. The detailed plans were revealed and final preparations, such as the waterproofing of vehicles and the issue of assault rations and French money, were completed. Embarkation began on 2 June at Southampton and convoys formed up in Southampton Water, Cowes Roads and the Solent, ready to sail during the afternoon and evening of 4 June. As is now well known, the invasion was delayed by twenty-four hours owing to storms in the Channel. Then, on the evening of 5 June, the weather was deemed good enough, though

Figure 5.15    *2nd Battalion The Hertfordshire Regiment – An N.C.O.s' cadre course parading for inspection in battledress, battle order, probably 1943. Other ranks, but not officers, are wearing the slip-on shoulder title shown in Figure 5.8 but have not been issued with formation patches or the scarlet infantry 'arm of service' strip. Note that only the front and centre ranks have the No. 4 rifle with spike bayonet, the rear ranks having the No. 3 with sword bayonet.*

(J. D. Sainsbury)

to the thousands of landsmen taking part it still seemed 'very rough', and the fleets set sail to arrive off their chosen beaches the following morning.

No. 9 Beach Group had been placed in support of 69 Infantry Brigade, one of the assault brigades of 50th (Northumbrian) Division, the leading division of XXX Corps on 'Gold' beach, which was the furthest west of the three beaches to be used by Twenty-First Army Group. The sector assigned to 69 Brigade was known as 'King' (divided into King Red and King Green) and No. 9 Beach Group was also to be responsible for the neighbouring 'Love Green' beach which was not used for the initial assault. No. 10 Beach Group was responsible for 'Jig' Sector of Gold beach, the western extremity of the British beaches, and together with No. 9 Beach Group made up 104 Beach Sub-Area. It is of interest to note that the only occasion during the two World Wars when a battalion of the Hertfordshire Regiment fought alongside a regiment of Hertfordshire's other major Territorial unit – the Hertfordshire Yeomanry – took place on King beach, for 86th (Hertfordshire Yeomanry) Field Regiment, Royal Artillery, a self-propelled field regiment, was in support of 69 Infantry Brigade throughout the landings, having taken part in a 'run-in' shoot on the enemy positions as their landing craft approached the beach. Follow-up details of the two Hertfordshire units actually travelled in the same landing craft.

The assault elements of 2nd Battalion got ashore at H+30 with minimal casualties after an 'uneventful, though unpleasant' crossing and C Company were almost immediately involved in street fighting in the village of La Rivière and in the neighbouring fixed defences and dug-outs. For some four hours the battalion was engaged in mopping up pockets of resistance along the beach westwards from La Rivière, including the coastal defence gun positions at Mont Fleury and Ver-sur-Mer, about one mile inland, which had been by-passed, according to plan, by the assault battalions, intent on pushing inland with minimum delay. Resistance was in some cases fierce but by mid-day the beach was secure apart from occasional activity by 'stay-behind' snipers.

During the afternoon of 'D' Day it became clear that the enemy were still in some strength in the hamlet of Vaux, about one-and-a-half miles south-east of La Rivière, and lying on the other side of the boundary between Gold and the Love sector of the neighbouring Canadian beach Juno. This position, which had been by-passed by the assault formations from both beaches, contained anti-tank guns which were harassing roads and tracks between the British and Canadian beaches. An attempt was made to over-run the area during daylight on 6 June. Naval gunfire support was arranged in the absence of artillery and B Company ordered to attack. The naval gunfire did not come down on time, and in attacking without support the company ran into heavy mortar fire and suffered some casualties. It was not possible to bring in either armoured or artillery support for a renewed assault immediately and the attack was called off as darkness fell. During the night a 40 mm anti-aircraft gun was moved from the beach defences to overlook the enemy near Vaux, and with covering fire from this gun and from part of D Company, B Company, reinforced by a platoon from D, carried the position soon after dawn on 7 June, leaving about forty enemy dead and taking over one hundred prisoners without further loss to the battalion. Isolated snipers remained and the battalion's whole area was not absolutely secure until D+3 (9 June).

Before full use could be made of the beaches a large proportion of the beach obstacles and mines had to be removed. The 2nd Battalion estimated that they were responsible for lifting some 12 000 mines – a valuable contribution to the beach group's overall effort, which was largely undertaken by the Royal Engineers. Two men from the assault pioneer platoon were killed during these operations.

The battalion soon settled down to the role of 'managing' the beaches, which were difficult to work in places as there were widespread patches of peat and clay which made vehicle movement very difficult. Nevertheless, No. 9 Beach Group claimed the Normandy Beaches record for the greatest numbers of men and vehicles and quantities of stores to pass over any one beach in one day. This included two thousand tons of stores, compared with an average daily throughput of stores of about fifteen hundred tons. By the middle of July 1944 the 'Mulberry' artificial harbour was beginning to operate at full capacity and movement across the beaches was nearing its end.

Their work with the beach group accomplished, the 2nd Battalion moved inland and began intensive training in the orthodox infantry role. Any hopes that they entertained of joining the victorious advance across North-West Europe were dashed in mid-August, however, when it was decided they were not to be used as a unit but would be broken up to provide reinforcements for other battalions – a sad end after years of waiting at home and a short but vital part in Operation Overlord. The battalion was accordingly dispersed but did not technically pass into suspended animation until mid-November 1944.

The long period of relative inactivity of both battalions in Home Forces provided the opportunity for officers and men to volunteer for apparently more adventurous postings and to volunteer or be selected 'without the option' for a wide range of other odd jobs – in official parlance, certainly as far as officers were concerned, 'extra-regimental employment' (or E.R.E). As a result, pre-war members of the 1st and 2nd Battalions ran into each other all over the world and accumulated individual experiences that could not possibly be fitted into a short history. It must, however, be recorded that some forty-five officers and men, approximately equally divided between the two battalions, were among the original volunteers for the Independent Companies, later world famous as the Commandos. No. 3 Independent Company was formed entirely from 54th Division, with each battalion providing a section of twenty men. After action in Norway in 1940 No. 3 Independent Company was absorbed into 1st Special Service Battalion, which was itself later divided to form Nos. 1 and 2 Commandos.

The award of the eight battle honours gained by the 1st and 2nd Battalions during the Second World War was not announced until May 1957.[2] All these honours were borne on the Queen's Colour of the 1st Battalion until 1961. They were:

'NORMANDY LANDING', 'NORTH-WEST EUROPE, 1944',
'MONTORSOLI', 'GOTHIC LINE', 'MONTE GAMBERALDI',
'MONTE CECO', 'MONTE GRANDE', 'ITALY, 1944–45'.

After amalgamation in 1961 all eight honours were borne on the Queen's Colour of the successor unit (see Chapter Six). It must be a matter for regret that neither they nor the 1st Battalion's Great War honours have yet been recognised and adopted by the Royal Anglian Regiment, of which the successors to the Hertfordshire Regiment now form part.

Fortunately the scale of loss in both killed and wounded did not approach that of First World War. Nevertheless, in just under six months' fighting in Italy the 1st Battalion lost one hundred all ranks killed in action or died of wounds, and as far as can be established the total number who lost their lives, including the 2nd Battalion's battle casualties and deaths from accident and illness was 135 all ranks. Steps are being taken to ensure that a revised regimental Roll of Honour for the Second World War is readily available for consultation both within the County and in London, since the regimental memorial in All Saints' Church, Hertford does not record the names of all those who lost their lives. Efforts are also being made to place on public record (other than in the *London Gazette*, which shows neither unit details nor citations) the names of the officers and men who were decorated or mentioned in despatches for gallantry or for distinguished service, both with the battalions and in E.R.E. posts.

## 5.4  1st Battalion 1947–1961

In discussions preceding the re-formation of the Territorial Army in 1947 the War Office first proposed that only one Territorial infantry battalion should be raised in the two counties of Hertfordshire and Bedfordshire, replacing the four battalions that had existed immediately before the war – 1st and 2nd Battalions The Hertfordshire Regiment and 5th and 6th Battalions The Bedfordshire and Hertfordshire Regiment. Battalion head-quarters of the post-war single battalion would have been in Bedfordshire and only two companies would have been based in Hertfordshire. Once again the proposal to remove Hertfordshire's own Territorial infantry unit from the *Army List* was vigorously resisted, with the result that it was agreed that a separate battalion should be raised in each county.

The 1st and 2nd Battalions of the Hertfordshire Regiment were amalga-mated in suspended animation and recruiting for the new county-wide 1st Battalion began in May 1947. By the end of the year sub-unit locations had been agreed as shown in Table 5.5. Changes in this organisation between 1947 and 1961 were few. The drill station at Bishop's Stortford was closed by 1950; No. 4 Company moved from Letchworth to Hitchin in 1955; and Support Company moved to Watford in 1956, when the mortar platoon at Ware was replaced by a platoon of No. 3 Company.

The 54th (East Anglian) Division, which had, as shown earlier, been broken up during the war, was not re-formed in 1947, although two of its original constituent brigades – 161 and 162 – were re-formed as indepen-dent infantry brigades. The 1st Battalion The Hertfordshire Regiment accordingly formed part of 162 Independent Infantry Brigade (Territorial

TABLE 5.5  *1st Battalion The Hertfordshire Regiment – 1947*

| | |
|---|---|
| Battalion Headquarters | Hertford |
| Headquarters Company | Hertford |
| Support Company<br>  Mortar Platoon | Hertford (less Mortar Platoon)<br>Ware |
| No. 1 Company | Hemel Hempstead (less one platoon)<br>St. Albans (one platoon) |
| No. 2 Company | Watford |
| No. 3 Company | Cheshunt (less one platoon)<br>Bishop's Stortford (one platoon) |
| No. 4 Company | Letchworth |
| Corps of Drums | Ware |

Figure 5.16 *1st Battalion The Hertfordshire Regiment – The first two recruits to enlist in the reconstituted battalion when recruiting opened in 1947.*

(Regimental collection)

Army) until October 1956 when the brigade losts its independence on joining the reconstituted 54th Division.

Throughout the period 1947–1961 the volunteer strength of the battalion, in common with other Territorial units, was low in comparison with establishment. On mobilisation numbers would have been made up by former National Servicemen who were posted to the battalion for the part-time element of their service. During the early 1950s these reservists were required to undertake some training with the battalion, normally including annual camp. The battalion thus consisted of a proportion of true Territorials who had signed on for volunteer engagements and a proportion of officers and men fulfilling compulsory obligations – not always a happy mixture and in marked contrast to the days of the all-volunteer battalion prior to 1939. As stocks of war-time vehicles and equipment dwindled, so the Territorial Army, understandably not first in line for new issues, began to fall quite seriously behind their Regular counterparts in overall 'fitness for war' – a problem which continued into the 1960s. The battalion was no exception to this general rule but the shortage of Territorial volunteers meant that the reduced numbers on weekend and annual training were not seriously inconvenienced by shortages, only by the increasing age of, for example, radio equipment.

The principal uniform was khaki serge battledress, worn for parades [98] and training. The white-on-red embroidered shoulder title 'Hertfordshire' was worn, together with the appropriate brigade or divisional cloth sign. Headgear was initially the general service cap, but this was replaced, to nobody's regret, by the blue beret, on which the 1st Battalion wore a scarlet patch under the original 1908 cap badge. Service dress of pre-war pattern was worn by officers 'in possession' and, following its introduction at the time of the Coronation in 1953, 'No. 1' dress could be obtained, at their own expense, by all ranks. The pattern worn by the battalion was standard for 'non-royal' infantry regiments, with cap and collar badges in gilt or gilding metal, as appropriate, and without any form of shoulder title.

Brigadier-General The Viscount Hampden, G.C.V.O., K.C.B., C.M.G. was succeeded as Honorary Colonel in 1949 by Colonel E. C. M. Phillips, C.B., D.S.O., T.D. After only a short tenure Colonel Phillips was succeeded by Brigadier J. A. Longmore, C.B., C.B.E., T.D., another former commanding officer of the 1st Battalion with a similarly distinguished career, in July 1952. Her Majesty The Queen (known after the accession of our present Queen in 1952 as Queen Elizabeth The Queen Mother)

Figure 5.17   *1st Battalion The Hertfordshire Regiment – Bandsmen in pre-1914 full dress sound a fanfare on the arrival of the judge at Hertford Assizes, 1951.*

(Regimental collection)

Figure 5.18 (Left)   *Colonel E. C. M. Phillips, C.B., D.S.O., T.D. (1883–1957) – First appointed to the 1st (Hertfordshire) Volunteer Battalion The Bedfordshire Regiment 1903; Commanding Officer 1st/1st Battalion The Hertfordshire Regiment August 1917 – March 1918 and 1st Battalion 1924–30; Honorary Colonel 1947–52.* (Bottom)   *1st Battalion The Hertfordshire Regiment – The Honorary Colonel inspects the battalion at camp prior to his retirement in 1952.*

(Regimental collection)

Figure 5.19  *1st Battalion The Hertfordshire Regiment – Skill-at-arms competition at Colchester, early 1950s. The warrant officers and sergeants seen here are wearing the khaki beret, shortly to be replaced by blue. Note also that the officers' cap badge is now polished gilt, rather than bronze.*

(Regimental collection)

Figure 5.20  *1st Battalion The Hertfordshire Regiment – The Coronation Detachment in No. 1 Dress, 1953.*

(Regimental collection)  [101]

Figure 5.21 *1st Battalion The Hertfordshire Regiment – The Regimental Band and Corps of Drums beat retreat in St. Mary's Square, Hitchin as part of the celebrations accompanying the Coronation of Her Majesty Queen Elizabeth II, June 1953.*

(Regimental collection)

continued as Honorary Colonel, and at a memorable ceremony held at County Hall, Hertford, on 25 October 1953 presented new Colours to the 1st Battalion and to the 5th Battalion The Bedfordshire and Hertfordshire Regiment. The 'Old Colours' of the 1st Battalion had been lodged in the safe-keeping of All Saints' Church, Hertford on the outbreak of war and restored to the care of the post-war 1st Battalion in November 1949. (The 2nd Battalion were entitled to Colours but had not had time to acquire them before mobilisation.) The 'New Colours' were evidently ordered before the change from 'King's' crown to 'Queen's' crown was approved and were thus identical in appearance to those they replaced, for the

Figure 5.22 *Lieutenant-Colonel I. W. S. Gray, T.D. (right), commanding officer of the 1st Battalion 1951–55, with his second-in-command and successor as commanding officer, Major R. A. Humbert, T.D. at annual camp in 1953. Note the formation sign of 162 Independent Infantry Brigade on Major Humbert's right sleeve.*

(Regimental collection)

Plate 2

*Queen's Colour*

1st Battalion The Hertfordshire Regiment

*Presented by Her Majesty Queen Elizabeth The Queen Mother at Hertford on 25 October 1953; battle honours for the Second World War added 1957; laid up in All Saints' Church, Hertford on 1 July 1967.*

(Specially drawn for this work by H. W. Gray, M.V.O.)

*Facing page 102*

Figure 5.23  *1st Battalion The Hertfordshire Regiment – The first boy soldiers to enlist in the battalion under the terms of A.C.I. 452/1953. Note the scarlet patch then worn behind the badge on the blue beret.*

(Regimental collection)

Figure 5.24  *1st Battalion The Hertfordshire Regiment – Her Majesty The Queen inspects a Guard of Honour found by the battalion at the start of her visit to Stevenage in April 1959. The guard commander is Major C. Simmons, who commanded the battalion from November 1959 to March 1961.*

(Regimental collection)

Figure 5.25 *1st Battalion The Hertfordshire Regiment – Drum major, No. 1 Dress, 1960.*

(Regimental collection)

regiment's battle honours for the Second World War had not yet been announced and could not be emblazoned on the new Queen's Colour.

Immediately after the announcement in Parliament in July 1960 that the Territorial Army was to be reorganised (see page 4) it became clear that the Hertfordshire Regiment was yet again under threat of removal from the *Army List*. The official plan was circulated during August as a new order of battle for 54th Division. The division would no longer be exclusively East Anglian but would include a London infantry brigade (56 Infantry Brigade) and some London divisional troops. The East Anglian infantry component was to be reduced to one brigade (161 Infantry Brigade), comprising four battalions, of which one was to be formed by amalgamation of the 1st Battalion The Hertfordshire Regiment and the 5th Battalion The Bedfordshire Regiment (as the 5th Battalion The Bedfordshire and Hertfordshire Regiment had been known since 1958).

The proposal was fiercely resisted by Hertfordshire Territorial and Auxiliary Forces Association, who were particularly concerned to retain one major unit recruited exclusively in Hertfordshire. They counterproposed an amalgamation of 286th (Hertfordshire Yeomanry) Field Regiment, Royal Artillery and 1st Battalion The Hertfordshire Regiment but no suitable role could be found for the new unit and, in any case, an amalgamation within Hertfordshire could only take place if a similar amalgamation took place within Bedfordshire, which also produced problems as to the role of the new Bedfordshire unit. The arguments were pressed throughout the summer and into the autumn but were ultimately unsuccessful – though success would not have saved the Hertfordshire Regiment's title – and the White Paper detailing the reorganisation , published in November 1960,[3] announced that the Bedfordshire Regiment and the Hertfordshire Regiment would amalgamate to form a Territorial battalion of the 3rd East Anglian Regiment (16th/44th Foot), the amalgamation and reorganisation to be completed by 1 May 1961.

Thus, after a century of continuous service, of expansion to meet the demands of war and contraction as each new peace reduced the call on the Auxiliary Forces, Hertfordshire's own infantry regiment, for so long a survivor despite the odds, was planned out of existence. The spirit of Hertfordshire's infantrymen was more difficult – indeed impossible – to extinguish, as the short history of successor units shows.

NOTES

1. A.O.s 481 and 482/1922
2. A.O. 47/1957
3. Cmnd. 1216

# Chapter 6

# *The Successors to The Hertfordshire Regiment*

## 6.1 1st Battalion The Bedfordshire and Hertfordshire Regiment 1961–1967

The plan for the reorganisation of the Territorial Army as detailed in the 1960 White Paper and amplified in part at sub-unit level by the revised 54th Division order of battle, provided for two major units to be recruited across the two counties of Hertfordshire and Bedfordshire – a field regiment of the Royal Artillery by amalgamation of 286th (Hertfordshire Yeomanry) Field Regiment and 305th (Bedfordshire Yeomanry) Light Regiment, and an infantry battalion by amalgamation of the 1st Battalion The Hertfordshire Regiment and the 5th Battalion The Bedfordshire Regiment. There was much still to be argued over during the closing months of 1960, notably the location of the headquarters of each unit and the proportion of sub-units to be raised in the 'other' county. Titles and badges came a little later.

Locations were decided largely on the basis of existing strengths. The dominant strength of the artillery lay in Bedfordshire, that of the infantry in Hertfordshire, and so it was eventually agreed that regimental headquarters, headquarters battery and one-and-a-half gun batteries of the new field regiment would be Bedfordshire-based, leaving only one-and-a-half batteries in Hertfordshire, while battalion headquarters, headquarters company and two rifle companies of the infantry battalion would be located in Hertfordshire and the remaining two rifle companies in Bedfordshire. The organisation agreed prior to formation, which did not change throughout the six-year life of the battalion, is shown in Table 6.1. The battalion formed on 1 April 1961, one month earlier than the target date set in the White Paper.

Although shown in the White Paper as a battalion of the 3rd East Anglian Regiment (16th/44th Foot) the new battalion did not in fact adopt the regimental designation. (Neither did the other Territorial battalion, the 4th/5th Battalion The Essex Regiment.) It was, however, shown immediately after the Regular battalion in the *Army List* and, with 4th/5th Battalion The Essex Regiment, under the overall heading '3rd East Anglian Regiment (16th/44th Foot), Territorial Army'. It was, if nothing else, logical that the new battalion should adopt a 'Bedfordshire and Hertfordshire' designation and the pressure from Hertfordshire for it to continue as 'The Hertfordshire Regiment' – a trade-off was suggested which allowed the amalgamated artillery regiment to keep the Bedfordshire Yeomanry title – was resisted. Accordingly the designation 'The Bedfordshire and Hertfordshire Regiment' was restored to the *Army List*, not without some complications, for the new regiment was not simply a resurrection of the old, as if from suspended animation, but incorporated additionally the history, traditions and 'spirit' of the Hertfordshire Regiment. The eventual agreement on the title 'The Bedfordshire and Hertfordshire Regiment'

apparently overlooked the fact that within infantry regiments battalions
are numbered even when they stand as the only one in being. The Territorial infantry in Hertfordshire had, for instance, always been the 1st
Battalion The Hertfordshire Regiment when only one battalion existed and

TABLE 6.1   *1st Battalion The Bedfordshire and Hertfordshire Regiment – 1961*

| | |
|---|---|
| Battalion Headquarters | Hertford |
| Headquarters Company | Hertford (less two platoons) |
| Reconnaissance Platoon | Ware |
| Assault Pioneer Platoon | Watford |
| No. 1 Company | Hemel Hempstead |
| No. 2 Company | Watford |
| No. 3 Company | Luton (less two platoons) |
| | Hitchin (one platoon) |
| | Dunstable (one platoon) |
| No. 4 Company | Bedford (less one platoon) |
| | Biggleswade (one platoon) |
| Corps of Drums | Ware |
| Band | Bedford |

further serially numbered battalions had been added on expansion. On
the intervention of the Colonel of the 3rd East Anglian Regiment steps
were taken in October 1961 to ensure that the new battalion was in future
properly designated as '1st Battalion The Bedfordshire and Hertfordshire
Regiment'.

Battle honours are awarded to an infantry regiment as a whole, not to
individual battalions, though of course battalions' claims can be seen and
identified by those with appropriate knowledge of their war histories. The
Hertfordshire Regiment, as has been made clear in previous chapters, was
a regiment consisting only of Territorial battalions. As a result their battle
honours reflected, apart from volunteer service in South Africa (see
page 46), mobilised service in the two World Wars only. The same was
not true of the Bedfordshire Regiment, who carried on their Regimental
Colour honours awarded to the Regular battalions of the 16th Foot for
battles starting with 'Namur, 1695' and on their Queen's Colour those
awarded to Regular, Special Reserve, Territorial and Service battalions for
the two World Wars. The new regiment carried all the honours of both
its predecessors but by happy chance the 5th Battalion was the only
battalion of the Bedfordshire (later Bedfordshire and Hertfordshire) Regiment in the various theatres for which it claimed honours and they can
thus readily be separated from the rest. It is of interest to list the honours
carried by the 'new', exclusively Territorial, Bedfordshire and Hertfordshire Regiment which were gained by their Territorial predecessors:

*3rd Volunteer Battalion The Bedfordshire Regiment*
*5th Battalion The Bedfordshire Regiment*
*5th and 6th Battalions The Bedfordshire and Hertfordshire Regiment*

'South Africa, 1900–02'

'SUVLA', 'Landing at Suvla', 'Scimitar Hill', 'Gallipoli, 1915', 'Egypt, 1915–17',
'GAZA', 'El Mughar', 'Nebi Samwil', 'Jerusalem', 'Jaffa', 'Tell 'Asur',
'Megiddo', 'Sharon', 'Palestine, 1917–18'.

'Singapore Island', 'Malaya, 1942'.

*1st and 2nd (Hertfordshire) Volunteer Battalions The Bedfordshire Regiment*
*1st and 2nd Battalions The Hertfordshire Regiment*

'South Africa, 1900–02'

'YPRES, 1914, '17', 'Nonne Bosschen', 'FESTUBERT, 1915', 'LOOS', 'SOMME, 1916, '18', 'Thiepval', 'Ancre Heights', 'ANCRE, 1916', 'PILCKEM', 'Menin Road', 'Polygon Wood', 'Broodseinde', 'Poelcappelle', 'Passchendaele', 'St. QUENTIN', 'Rosières', 'Lys', 'Kemmel', 'Albert, 1918', 'Bapaume, 1918', 'HINDENBURG LINE', 'Havrincourt', 'Cambrai, 1918', 'Selle', 'SAMBRE', 'FRANCE AND FLANDERS, 1914–18'.

'NORMANDY LANDING', 'NORTH-WEST EUROPE, 1944', 'MONTORSOLI', 'GOTHIC LINE', 'MONTE GAMBERALDI', 'MONTE CECO', 'MONTE GRANDE', 'ITALY, 1944–45'.

A commitee of serving officers and retired officers of the two predecessor battalions was convened following the amalgamation to recommend appropriate badges and other details of uniform for the new regiment. The committee did not favour the use of the badges of the earlier Bedfordshire and Hertfordshire Regiment but selected from a variety of possible designs for the new cap badge (and the badge to be carried on the Regimental Colour), one which incorporated the traditional 'eagle and castle' of the Borough of Bedford earlier used by the Bedfordshire Rifle Volunteers and the 'hart lodged' of the Hertfordshire Regiment (Figure 6.1 *Left*). They further selected the hart collar badge of the Hertfordshire Regiment with the title scroll removed (Figure 6.1 *Centre*) and the button of the earlier Bedfordshire and Hertfordshire Regiment incorporating the hart trippant (Figure 6.1 *Right*). The white-on-scarlet embroidered shoulder title 'Bedfordshire and Hertfordshire' was resurrected for wear in battle-

Figure 6.1  *The Bedfordshire and Hertfordshire Regiment (1961–71) – (Left) Officer's gilt and silver plate cap badge approved in 1961 and incorporating the eagle and castle of the Borough of Bedford and the hart lodged of the Hertfordshire Regiment. A similar badge in anodised aluminium was worn by other ranks. (Actual size 30 mm. × 40 mm.) (Centre) Officer's gilt collar badge based on that previously worn by the Hertfordshire Regiment (see Figure 4.2). (Actual size 28 mm. × 28 mm.)*
                                                                                (J. D. Sainsbury)
*(Right) Design for a button similar to that worn by the Bedfordshire and Hertfordshire Regiment between 1919 and 1957 and taken into use by the 'new' Bedfordshire and Hertfordshire Regiment in 1961. (Diameter 24 mm.)*
                                                                        (Regimental collection)

Figure 6.2 *1st Battalion The Bedfordshire and Hertfordshire Regiment – Her Majesty the Queen inspects a Guard of Honour found by the battalion during her visit to Luton in November 1962. The guard commander is wearing the new cap and collar badges approved for the regiment but they have not yet been issued to other ranks.*

(Regimental collection)

dress, which continued as the authorised parade uniform. No. 1 Dress ('Blues') was still worn at individuals' expense.

For just over two years the battalion held the Colours of both their predecessors. These were paraded for the last time at a ceremony at Luton Hoo on 13 July 1963 when Her Majesty Queen Elizabeth The Queen Mother, Colonel-in-Chief of the 3rd East Anglian Regiment, presented new Colours, the new Queen's Colour bearing the combined 1914–18 and 1939–45 battle honours of the former Bedfordshire and Hertfordshire Regiment and the Hertfordshire Regiment, thirty-two in all, and the Regimental Colour the seven ancient battle honours of 'The Peacemakers' and 'South Africa 1900–02' (Figure 6.5). The old Colours of the 1st Battalion The Hertfordshire Regiment were laid up in All Saints' Church, Hertford, beside those presented in 1909 (see page 51) on 1 July 1967.

The battalion went to its first camp in 1961 three-hundred strong and carried out orthodox infantry training. In keeping with the increased attention given to Civil Defence, now a recognised role of the Territorial Army, camp in 1962 was at the Civil Defence Training Centre at Millom, Cumberland – in fact the only such camp in the battalion's short history. Within [109]

Figure 6.3  *1st Battalion The Bedfordshire and Hertfordshire Regiment – (Top) Civil Defence rescue training on a local building site, early 1962. (Centre) The 7.62-mm. self-loading rifle in use shortly after issue to the battalion in 1962. (Bottom) Vickers medium machine-gun practice at annual camp, June 1964. Note the embroidered white-on-red 'Bedfordshire and Hertfordshire' shoulder title worn on battledress and the East Anglian Brigade flash on the left sleeve.*

(Regimental collection)

Figure 6.4 (On facing page)  *1st Battalion The Bedfordshire and Hertfordshire Regiment – Presentation of New Colours to the battalion at Luton Hoo, July 1963. Her Majesty Queen Elizabeth The Queen Mother, Colonel-in-Chief of the Third East Anglian Regiment, inspects the parade (Top). The Old Colours march off, those of the 5th Battalion The Bedfordshire and Hertfordshire Regiment leading (Bottom left). Her Majesty presents the Regimental Colour (Bottom right).*

(© Luton News)

[111]

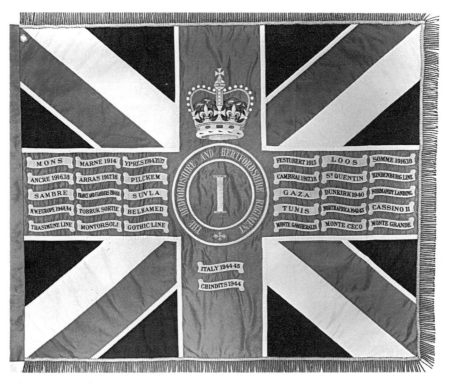

Figure 6.5   *1st Battalion The Bedfordshire and Hertfordshire Regiment – Queen's Colour* (Top) *and Regimental Colour* (Bottom) *made by Hobson and Sons of London and presented to the battalion by H.M. Queen Elizabeth The Queen Mother at Luton Hoo on 13 July 1963. The battle honours formerly carried by the Bedfordshire and Hertfordshire Regiment and by the Hertfordshire Regiment are borne on the New Colours (see page 107).*

(© Photograph by A. R. Tuck/A. C. K. Ware Ltd. for Hobson and Sons)

a fortnight of formation, on 13 April 1961, the battalion found a guard of honour for Her Majesty Queen Elizabeth The Queen Mother during her visit to St. Albans. On 2 November 1962 they found a guard of honour for Her Majesty The Queen at Luton. As can be seen in Figure 6.2, on neither occasion were the badges of the new regiment available, with the result that both guards presented a somewhat 'piebald' appearance, with both counties' old cap badges being worn.

With the incorporation of the 3rd East Anglian Regiment into the Royal Anglian Regiment in September 1964, the 1st Battalion The Bedfordshire and Hertfordshire Regiment became affiliated to the Royal Anglian Regiment and took precedence as the fifth Territorial battalion, without change in title or badges. (Indeed, at this time none of the affiliated Territorial units of the Royal Anglian Regiment became Territorial battalions of the regiment.)

The new affiliation had barely had time to take effect when it became clear early in 1965 that a very far-reaching reform of the Territorial Army was about to take place, and that the survival of even a sub-unit of infantry in Hertfordshire to carry on the history and traditions of the Hertfordshire Regiment was by no means guaranteed. The intention was to raise many fewer units, only thirteen of them infantry battalions, and to concentrate them in cities and towns where the prospect of recruiting to full establishment was judged to be greater. All this was to be accomplished within the existing availability of training centres ('drill halls'). On this basis it was unlikely that Hertfordshire would be allocated the task of raising any infantry. The situation was saved as far as the county was concerned by the decision to retain a 'Territorial Force for Home Service', in addition to the units already announced in the White Paper, which in general would move to the continent on mobilisation (see page 5). It was announced in May 1966 that the Bedfordshire and Hertfordshire Regiment would be among those units that would be retained with a Home Service role. Extinction had been avoided but the next two years were to be the most difficult that the infantry of Hertfordshire had faced in peace-time.

## 6.2   The Bedfordshire and Hertfordshire Regiment (Territorial) 1967–1971

The 1st Battalion The Bedfordshire and Hertfordshire Regiment was transferred to Category III of the Territorial and Army Volunteer Reserve on 1 April 1967 and designated The Bedfordshire and Hertfordshire Regiment (Territorial). On transfer the regiment absorbed part of 286th (Hertfordshire and Bedfordshire Yeomanry) Field Regiment, Royal Artillery and the incorporation of the Yeomanry (which also had another successor unit – 201 Medium Battery, Royal Artillery) was recognised in two of the sub-unit titles authorised by Army Order 14 of 1967. The new regiment had an establishment of four rifle companies – one more than the normal establishment for a Category III unit. There was no headquarters company but reconnaissance, signals and pioneer platoons provided specialist services. The reorganisation resulted in some changes of station as compared with the stations of the 1st Battalion between 1961 and 1967, as shown in Table 6.2 There were no out-lying detachments and the drill halls at Watford and Ware were closed.

Uniform, badges and buttons were those of the predecessor unit. Certain differences were adopted, however, by the two Yeomanry companies. Gold anodised aluminium shoulder titles 'H.Y.' and 'B.Y.'

TABLE 6.2    *The Bedfordshire and Hertfordshire Regiment (Territorial) – 1967*

| | |
|---|---|
| Regimental Headquarters | Hertford |
| Reconnaissance Platoon, Signals Platoon and Corps of Drums | Hertford |
| Pioneer Platoon | Bedford |
| No. 1 (Hertford) Company | Hertford |
| No. 2 (Hertfordshire Yeomanry) Company | Hemel Hempstead |
| No. 3 (Bedfordshire Yeomanry) Company | Luton |
| No. 4 (Bedfordshire) Company | Bedford |

were authorised for wear by Nos. 2 and 3 Companies respectively[1] but were not in fact produced before the regiment was disbanded. The Yeomanry companies also wore mounted pattern No. 1 Dress with steel shoulder chains. The regiment continued to carry the Colours presented to the 1st Battalion The Bedfordshire and Hertfordshire Regiment in 1963.

Category III units were visibly 'poor relations' of those in Categories I and II. Differences were marked from the start, with Category III units equipped, for instance, with the No. 4 rifle and dressed in battledress while Category II units were quickly issued with the 7.62 mm self-loading rifle and combat dress. Enthusiasts kept going but it proved difficult to attract recruits and, with only an eight-day annual camp and four other paid training days in the year it must be doubtful whether recruits could have been trained effectively. Nevertheless, in common with similar units all over the country, the Bedfordshire and Hertfordshire Regiment struggled on. In May 1968 a Ministry of Defence instruction informed Category III units that, after only a year's existence, their future was under scrutiny. Meanwhile they could continue to train without any cost to public funds. It was, of course, impossible to train at no cost, and the regiment had to raise funds, resorting to jumble sales and raffles, and charging members for attendance at weekends and at camp rather than paying them. In the face of all these difficulties the Bedfordshire and Hertfordshire Regiment managed to organise a highly successful week's camp in Guernsey in September 1968 – perhaps the most enterprising undertaking by any unit.

Once authority was given in November 1968 for the raising in Hertfordshire of an additional company for 5th (Volunteer) Battalion The Royal Anglian Regiment (see below) interest in the Hertfordshire companies of the Bedfordshire and Hertfordshire Regiment almost collapsed. No such competition was introduced in Bedfordshire but it must have been with some relief, albeit with some distress too, that the cadre, sponsored by 5th (Volunteer) Battalion, was formed on 1 February 1969. Handover to the cadre was completed by 31 March, when the Bedfordshire and Hertfordshire Regiment (Territorial) was disbanded.

For some time the idea was maintained officially that the cadre represented the old Volunteer and Territorial infantry of both counties but this idea proved particularly difficult to sustain in Hertfordshire, where No. 5 Company, 5th (Volunteer) Battalion The Royal Anglian Regiment was fast assuming the mantle of successor unit to the Hertfordshire Regiment. On 1 April 1971 B Company, 6th (Volunteer) Battalion The Royal Anglian Regiment began to form at Bedford. With infantry sub-units now in both counties it was deemed that the cadre had discharged its task of providing the nucleus around which new units could be formed and of safeguarding the Colours and property of the Bedfordshire and Hertfordshire Regiment. It was accordingly disbanded on the eve of the formation of 6th (Volunteer) Battalion on 31 March 1971. The Colours were handed over to the 6th (Volunteer) Battalion and were paraded for the last time on 24 June 1979 (in common with those of the 4th Battalion The Royal Norfolk Regiment, The Suffolk and Cambridgeshire Regiment and the 4th/5th Battalion The Essex Regiment) when, as the 'Old Colours', they were marched off and H.R.H. The Princess Margaret presented New Colours to the 6th (Volunteer) Battalion. The Colours of the 1st Battalion The Bedfordshire and Hertfordshire Regiment were laid up in St. Albans Abbey on 19 October 1980.

Meanwhile, a new list of T. & A.V.R. successor units to Territorial Army units had been published.[2] It showed officially for the first time that the successors of the Bedfordshire and Hertfordshire Regiment, Territorial Army, were No. 5 (Hertfordshire) Company, 5th (Volunteer) Battalion The Royal Anglian Regiment and B (Bedfordshire) Company, 6th (Volunteer) Battalion The Royal Anglian Regiment. The local interpretation, to which no objection need be taken, is that the succession of the Volunteer and Territorial infantry in Hertfordshire rests with No. 5 Company (which has since been redesignated – see below), while that in Bedfordshire rests with B Company. The short-lived Bedfordshire and Hertfordshire Regiment, 1961–1971, described above, thus provides the bridge between the Hertfordshire Regiment and their present-day successors as Hertfordshire's Volunteer infantry.

### 6.3 No. 4 (Hertfordshire) Company, 5th (Volunteer) Battalion The Royal Anglian Regiment

A single battalion of the Royal Anglian Regiment was raised in Category IIA of the Territorial and Army Volunteer Reserve in April 1967. Designated 5th (Volunteer) Battalion, its four rifle companies reflected the existing organisation of the Royal Anglian Regiment in four Regular battalions. Each Volunteer company was 'associated' with the Regular battalion from its recruiting area and wore its battalion collar badge, thus:

| Volunteer Company | Company Locations | Associated Regular Battalion |
|---|---|---|
| No. 1 (Norfolk and Suffolk) Company | Lowestoft/Ipswich | 1st Battalion |
| No. 2 (Duchess of Gloucester's Own Lincolnshire and Northamptonshire) Company | Lincoln/Gainsborough | 2nd Battalion |
| No. 3 (16th/44th Foot) Company | Chelmsford/Colchester | 3rd Battalion |
| No. 4 (Leicestershire) Company | Leicester/Loughborough | 4th Battalion |

It can be seen that at this stage, although perhaps notionally linked with No. 3 Company, Hertfordshire was not represented in the battalion, the only representative of the long line of Hertfordshire's Volunteer and Territorial infantry then being No. 1 Company of the Bedfordshire and Hertfordshire Regiment (Territorial) (see above).

In November 1968 (see page 6) it was announced that a number of former Category IIA units, now known as 'Group A' units, including 5th

(Volunteer) Battalion The Royal Anglian Regiment, would be authorised, from 1 January 1969, to recruit to 140 per cent of establishment. It was decided that part of 5th Battalion's extra 40 per cent would be used to raise a new company of two rifle platoons only (compared with the normal three), together with one of the battalion's two anti-tank platoons, in Hertfordshire. The new company, designated No. 5 (16th/44th Foot) Company took over the drill halls and many of the members of the two Hertfordshire companies of the Bedfordshire and Hertfordshire Regiment (Territorial), then in process of disbanding and handing over to its representative cadre, which was to be sponsored by 5th (Volunteer) Battalion. Company Headquarters and 13 Platoon were formed at Hertford while 14 Platoon and the Anti-tank Platoon, equipped with four of the battalion's eight 120 mm 'Mobat' anti-tank guns were at Hemel Hempstead. (The decision whether to retain the battalion support weapons within headquarters company or to group them with rifle companies rested with each Volunteer battalion and there were several different solutions reflecting, for example, recruiting potential and facilities for storage and maintenance of technical equipment.)

On 30 March 1969, the day before the Bedfordshire and Hertfordshire Regiment (Territorial) was due to disband, a 're-badging' parade was held at Hertford, at which members of the newly-formed company exchanged their old cap and collar badges for the cap badge of the Royal Anglian Regiment and the 'Salamanca eagle' collar badge of 3rd Battalion The Royal Anglian Regiment. The company also adopted the black and amber lanyard formerly worn by the Bedfordshire and Hertfordshire Regiment but this has since been exchanged for the 'Pompadour' purple lanyard of 3rd Battalion The Royal Anglian Regiment. It is worth noting that, with effect from 1 June 1969, the Regular battalions of the Royal Anglian Regiment discarded their individual collar badges in favour of a universal regimental pattern. It had been intended that the Volunteer companies should follow this practice but none did so and they were still wearing their company collar badges when battalion collar badges were restored to the Regular battalions in 1980. It is also noticeable that the subsidiary title '16th/44th Foot' rested uncomfortably upon a company whose predecessors had, as described earlier, fought so hard for the greatest possible independence from the 16th Foot – The Bedfordshire Regiment. No. 5 Company began using the description 'Bedfordshire and Hertfordshire', in 1970, when there was no Volunteer infantry in Bedfordshire. In 1971, when 6th (Volunteer) Battalion The Royal Anglian Regiment was raised, the 'Bedfordshire' part of the title was transferred to B (Bedfordshire) Company of the 6th Battalion. Thereafter the Hertfordshire Company of 5th Battalion used the bracketed designation 'Hertfordshire', though formal approval of this practice was not given until February 1980.

Throughout 1969, which saw No. 5 Company at its first annual camp with the battalion and was, in general a year in which firm foundations were laid, the company did not legally exist. Personnel and equipment were held under the battalion's overall increased ceilings and, as it were, just 'happened' to be organised as a company and located in Hertfordshire. Other battalions had taken similar action to raise additional sub-units and all these were given official recognition with effect from 15 December 1969. The last step in the chain of events which led to No. 5 Company assuming officially the mantle of a successor unit to the Bedfordshire and Hertfordshire Regiment (Territorial), and, by extension, to the Hertfordshire Regiment and the earlier Rifle Volunteers, was taken on 31 March 1971 when

Figure 6.6 *5th (Volunteer) Battalion The Royal Anglian Regiment – Her Majesty Queen Elizabeth The Queen Mother presenting Colours to the battalion at Tidworth, 12 July 1974.*

(© Soldier)    [117]

Figure 6.7 *Anti-tank Platoon, 5th (Volunteer) Battalion The Royal Anglian Regiment – A Milan anti-tank guided weapon detachment running into action during weekend training.*

(© E. Collinson, Cambridge)

Figure 6.8 *The Royal Anglian Regiment – (Left) Cap badge. (Right) Collar badge worn by the 3rd Battalion and 'associated' companies (raised in Bedfordshire, Hertfordshire and Essex) of the 5th and 6th (Volunteer) Battalions.*

Figure 6.9   No. 4 Company, 5th (Volunteer) Battalion The Royal Anglian Regiment on Exercise 'Lionheart' in Germany, 1984. (Top) A patrol led by a soldier carrying the 7.62 mm self-loading rifle with 'individual weapon sight', which provides a degree of magnification and improved night vision. The belt-fed 'general purpose machine-gun', successor to the Bren gun (Figure 5.19) can also be seen. (Right) A signaller in full nuclear, biological and chemical protective equipment.
(© Hertfordshire Mercury)

the Cadre of the Bedfordshire and Hertfordshire Regiment (Territorial) was disbanded. The following day B (Bedfordshire) Company of 6th (Volunteer) Battalion was raised and the succession of Volunteer and Territorial infantry in the two counties devolved separately upon No. 5 Company and B Company – a fact eventually confirmed by a revised Succession Warrant.[2]

The designation 'No. 5 Company' and the establishment of two rifle platoons with an anti-tank platoon was relatively short-lived. An extensive reorganisation of the British Army of the Rhine and the 'N.A.T.O.-roled' units, both Regular and Volunteer, based in the United Kingdom but scheduled to move to the continent as reinforcements, took place during the winter of 1977–78 with an effective date of 1 April 1978. Two Volunteer battalions of the Royal Anglian Regiment – 5th and 7th Battalions – were from this date included in the order of battle of 7th Field Force – a mixed Regular/Volunteer formation equivalent in earlier terminology to a reinforced brigade – with the task on mobilisation of moving swiftly to Germany to fight as part of I (British) Corps. This revised role (which for 7th Battalion entailed transfer from 'General Reserve' to 'N.A.T.O.') required considerable restructuring of both battalions (described fully in *A Guide to the History of the Bedfordshire and Hertfordshire Regiment*), which resulted in 5th Battalion being reduced to the normal infantry battalion establishment of four rifle companies. The original No. 4 Company, recruited in Leicestershire, was transferred to 7th Battalion and No. 5 Company was moved up to fill the gap and redesignated No. 4 Company. At the same time the company was brought up to full establishment of three rifle platoons with platoons numbered 10, 11 and 12. The anti-tank platoon remained 'grouped' with No. 4 Company. The organisation of the company and locations of platoons at the time of writing are:

| | |
|---|---|
| Company Headquarters 10 (East Herts) Platoon 11 (Mid-Herts) Platoon | Hertford |
| 12 (West Herts) Platoon Anti-Tank Platoon | Hemel Hempstead |

On 1 January 1982, as part of a further restructuring of the British Army of the Rhine, and notably of the 'front-line' formations in I (British) Corps, the 5th (Volunteer) Battalion joined the newly-formed 49 Infantry Brigade as part of 2nd Infantry Division. The division is tasked on mobilisation with the defence of the 'corps rear area' and consists at present of one Regular brigade – 24 Infantry Brigade – and two Territorial brigades – 15 and 49 Infantry Brigades. The division is based entirely in the United Kingdom and both Regular and Territorial elements would thus depend upon timely and swift movement to their battle positions on the Continent in the event of mobilisation.

The present-day Territorial Army provides over 30 per cent of the United Kingdom's land forces, and units are required to mobilise, whether for service on the Continent or in defence of the United Kingdom base, with a full complement of trained officers and men within a handful of days – a very different situation from that obtaining before the outbreak of the Second World War, when it was assumed that Territorial formations would be able to train for some months after mobilisation and before being committed to battle. N.A.T.O.–roled units exercise abroad, normally in Germany, and often as part of higher level formation training, every two or three years. No. 4 Company is no exception and did its first annual camp in Germany in 1970. It took part in the huge reinforcement exercises 'Crusader' in 1980 and 'Lion Heart' in 1984, each in its turn the biggest exercise that the British Army has held in peace time. In 1985 the company was selected to spend its annual camp in Gibraltar, exchanging with a company of the resident battalion, 1st Battalion The Queen's Regiment. Like their predecessors in 1943–44 (see page 77) the company scrambled around the Rock on exercises and even provided the guard at Government House. During this short tour members of the Hertfordshire Regiment Old Comrades Association visited No. 4 Company, and veterans and young serving soldiers were able to compare notes on their experiences in the Fortress Garrison.

It has been almost customary for the serving Volunteer, now Territorial, to claim throughout the 130 or so years of Hertfordshire's Volunteer infantry that he and his comrades have reached a higher pitch of efficiency than any of their predecessors. Doubtless the predecessors contest the claim and the argument, nearly always good humoured, will fortunately never be resolved. Meanwhile, No. 4 Company, visibly better armed and equipped than any previous generation, are without doubt worthy successors to the history, traditions and achievements of the Hertfordshire Regiment.

NOTES

1. Army Dress Committee Decision 1859/1967

2. D.C.I. (Army) S 17/1976

# Chapter 7

# *Affiliated Units and Sub-Units*

## 7.1 The Veteran Reserve/The National Reserve 1910–1916

Formation of the Veteran Reserve was authorised, and regulations for the Reserve published, in May 1910.[1] It was to consist of officers and men who had served in any of the military forces of the Crown but had no further liability for recall to the colours in the event of general mobilisation. In war, according to the original regulations, the Reserve was to 'fulfil, in connection with local defence . . . miscellaneous functions demanding from those who undertake them a spirit of military discipline and some knowledge of the use of arms'. County Territorial Force Associations were charged with the formation and organisation of the Reserve in their own counties. Neither uniform nor arms were issued in peace-time but arrangements were made for members to undertake rifle practice locally. The title was changed to 'National Reserve' in 1911.[2] Revised regulations published in 1911[3] and 1913[4] developed the role and character of the Reserve so that by 1913 members were divided into three classes: Class 1 – Officers and men whose age and medical category fitted them for service 'in the field' at home and abroad and who undertook an 'honourable obligation' to rejoin H.M. Forces in time of imminent national danger; Class II – Officers and men whose age and medical category fitted them for home defence or duty in fixed positions or for administrative work, and who undertook a similar obligation; and Class III – those who were qualified for Classes I and II but were not willing to undertake the obligation or those not qualified (normally on age grounds) for Classes I and II. It was planned that on presenting themselves on mobilisation members of Classes I and II would be posted as reinforcements to Regular or mobilised Territorial units and to strengthen garrisons, guard vulnerable points, or be employed as specialists or tradesmen in technical branches or in hospital, veterinary, remount, clerical, recruiting or other military duties.

On mobilisation in 1914 those members of the National Reserve who were not directed as individual reinforcements were commissioned or enlisted into the Territorial Force and formed into Supernumerary Territorial Force Companies to provide additional organised manpower for the guarding of railways and other vulnerable points in the United Kingdom.[5] These companies consisted of 120 all ranks. Each was affiliated to a Territorial battalion raised in the same county and any designation reflecting origin in the National Reserve was discarded. Later some individuals who were fit and available for 'more active military work' were formed into composite battalions which were designated 18th – 24th Battalions The Rifle Brigade.[6] These depletions, together with individuals re-enlisting into the Regular Army or transferring to Provisional Home Service Battalions (T.F.) led to a reorganisation of Supernumerary Companies and reduction in their numbers.[7] Finally, in March–April 1916, existing Supernumary Companies were absorbed into the newly-formed Royal Defence Corps

Figure 7.1  *National Reserve – Lapel badge,*
*gilt and blue enamel, worn by members of the*
*National Reserve enrolled in Hertfordshire,*
*1910–1914. (Actual size 22 mm. × 28 mm.)*
(J. D. Sainsbury)

and all individual county connections were lost, even though Protection Companies of the Royal Defence Corps were recognised as the successor units to Supernumerary Territorial Force Companies.[8] The National Reserve was formally abolished in January 1922.[9]

Four companies, designated Nos. 1, 2, 3 and 4 Supernumerary Companies, 1st Battalion The Hertfordshire Regiment, were formed from officers and men of the National Reserve who reported for duty in Hertfordshire. No details of their employment are recorded but it is known that their combined strength in March–April 1916 was still just over three hundred all ranks, of whom 275 transferred to the Royal Defence Corps. The buttonhole badge issued for wear in civilian clothes by members of the National Reserve registered with Hertfordshire Territorial Force Association is shown in Figure 7.1.

## 7.2  The Volunteer Training Corps/The Volunteer Force 1914–1919

In November 1914 the government decided to exert a degree of control over the local volunteer units which were being formed throughout the country. The Central Association of Volunteer Training Corps was accordingly set up and local units were required to become affiliated to the Association and conform to its regulations. One of the effects of the tighter control was the grouping of local units from towns and villages into battalions, for both administrative and tactical convenience. Another was the universal adoption of an approved pattern of uniform. Lovat green twill, or later serge, was used, following the requirement that the uniform should be easily distinguishable from that of the Regular forces. All ranks wore a scarlet brassard with the letters 'G.R.' on the left arm. As a further measure designed to set the Volunteer Training Corps apart from His

Majesty's Forces, officers were not commissioned, but merely appointed and the use of the normal military ranks was not permitted.

In April 1916 the government at last took advantage of existing volunteer legislation (the Volunteer Acts, 1863–1900) to accept the offers of the Volunteer Training Corps to serve in the country's defence. The lovat green uniform was then recognised as belonging to an arm of His Majesty's Forces, the red brassard was discarded and the Volunteer Training Corps was renamed the Volunteer Force. Regulations for the Volunteer Force were issued and County Territorial Force Associations were asked to take over the administration of units raised in their areas. In September 1916 the officers of the Volunteer Force were gazetted to commissions in the Force, and ranks were brought into line with the army. Khaki uniforms began to be issued in December 1916. The final change in the constitution of the Volunteer Force came in July 1918 when Volunteer regiments were permitted to style themselves Volunteer battalions of their local Regular or Territorial regiment.[10] The majority adopted the alternative title and the badges of their affiliated regiments.

The Volunteer Training Corps was, from its inception, intended to supplement the full-time forces in the defence of the United Kingdom against invasion, but increasingly members of the Corps wanted to take a more active part in other aspects of Home Defence. Although some did so unofficially it was not until the autumn of 1916 that the authorities decided the Volunteers could contribute to manpower savings, and units were tasked with guards on vulnerable points and at prisoner-of-war camps and other suitable duties. Additional legislation was required and was passed in December 1916 as the Volunteer Act, 1916. In the very difficult spring and summer of 1918, when enemy raids were still feared yet every possible man was required at the front, the government took special steps to enable the Volunteers to serve for limited periods of full-time duty. As there was no invasion, units could not be called up but they provided composite companies of individual volunteers, known as Special Service Companies, for duty on the threatened East Coast of the United Kingdom.

The Hertfordshire Volunteer Regiment was formed under the auspices of the Central Association in May 1915 and took under command over twenty local units that had already been formed in the county. The regiment consisted initially of four battalions, but some difficulty was experienced in obtaining the necessary volunteers from the Barnet area to secure the independence of the 4th Battalion, and in 1916 it was absorbed into the 3rd Battalion as a single company. The organisation of the regiment, which had a small headquarters at Hatfield, was then as shown in Table 7.1.

Except for the addition of No. 5 Company (Berkhamsted) to the 2nd

TABLE 7.1　*Hertfordshire Volunteer Regiment – 1916*

|  | 1st Battalion (East Hertfordshire) | 2nd Battalion (West Hertfordshire) | 3rd Battalion (Mid-Hertfordshire) |
|---|---|---|---|
| Battalion Headquarters | Hertford | Watford | St. Albans |
| No. 1 Company | Bishop's Stortford | Watford | St. Albans |
| No. 2 Company | Hitchin | Chorleywood | Barnet |
| No. 3 Company | Hertford | Bushey Heath | Harpenden |
| No. 4 Company | Letchworth and Royston | Hemel Hempstead | Hatfield |

Figure 7.2 *Hertfordshire Volunteer Regiment – Officer's bronze finish cap badge adopted by the 1st Battalion and later extended to the 2nd and 3rd Battalions. The same badge was used as an officer's collar badge and, in brass, as the other ranks' cap badge. (Actual size 43 mm. × 36 mm.) (Centre) All ranks' cap badge, polished gilt on matt black, adopted by the 2nd Battalion in May 1915. (Actual size 36 mm. × 43 mm.) (Right) Other ranks' brass shoulder title. (Actual size 52 mm. × 27 mm.)*

(J. D. Sainsbury)

Battalion during 1917, this organisation obtained until stand-down. The strength of the regiment reached a peak of 2700 all ranks in February 1917 but by the spring of 1918 numbers had fallen to about 1600 and measures were in hand to bring about the amalgamation of the three battalions into one. The raising of a special service company, designated No. 8 (Hertfordshire) Special Service Company, diverted attention from the proposed amalgamation, which never took place. No. 8 Special Service Company reached a strength of only just over ninety all ranks, compared with its establishment of 114, but was nevertheless embodied and served for three months from 29 June 1918 on the Essex coast. Two members of the company died on full-time service. Recruiting and compulsory drills ceased in December 1918 but formal disbandment did not start until September of the following year and was completed in March 1920.

The 1st and 3rd Battalions of the Hertfordshire Volunteer Regiment wore a cap badge based on the 'hart lodged' of the Hertfordshire Regiment (Figure 7.2 *left*) until all regiments were ordered to replace their individual badges by the universal Royal Arms cap badge in April 1917. The 2nd Battalion's badge was of entirely new design (Figure 7.2 *Centre*). The metal shoulder title 'HERTS V.R.' was worn by all three battalions. The regiment took advantage of the change of title authorised in July 1918 and the three battalions were redesignated 1st, 2nd and 3rd Volunteer Battalions The Hertfordshire Regiment. Hertfordshire Regiment cap badges were adopted following this change and the shoulder title, which was by then embroidered to save metal, was altered to 'V. HERTS'. Officers wore a 'V' beneath the Hertfordshire Regiment officers' collar badge.

## 7.3 The Defence Force 1921

The threat to public order during the 1921 coal miners' strike was judged to be so great that the government called out the Regular Army Reserve and made extensive preparations to back civil power by military. It was thought to be unwise to order embodiment of the Territorial Force, but further troops were needed and on 8 April the Prime Minister appealed to loyal citizens to enlist for a temporary period of full-time service, not to exceed ninety days, with the Regular Army in new units to be called Defence Units. Enlistment, which was for service in the United Kingdom only, was open to those discharged from military service; to serving [125]

Figure 7.3  *2nd (West Herts) Battalion The Hertfordshire Volunteer Regiment – Battalion parade at The Grove, Watford, May 1915. All ranks are wearing the Norfolk jacket version of the grey-green uniform with the cap badge shown in Figure 7.1 (Centre). The rifles are 'gas pipe' dummies.*
(J. D. Sainsbury)

Figure 7.4  *1st (East Herts) Battalion The Hertfordshire Volunteer Regiment – Week-end training in February 1916, shortly before the change to the Royal Arms cap badge. They are wearing the service dress style of grey-green uniform and the cap badge shown in Figure 7.2 (Right). The 'GR' brassard can be seen on the left arm of the officer in the foreground.*
(J. D. Sainsbury)

Figure 7.5  *1st Volunteer Battalion The Hertfordshire Regiment – A smart group of signallers with an officer, late 1918. The officer is wearing khaki service dress with the bronze cap and collar badges of the Hertfordshire Regiment (Figure 4.2) and the letter 'V' on the collar. Other ranks are wearing khaki serge service dress with the cloth title V/HERTS sewn to the top of the sleeve, rather than on the shoulder strap. They have not yet been issued with Hertfordshire Regiment cap badges.*

(Private collection)

officers and men of the Territorial Force; and to certain categories of civilians with specialist qualifications.

Units of the Defence Force were based on Territorial drill halls, and large numbers of serving officers and men joined the Force. Their commissions or engagements in the Territorial Force were deemed to have lapsed on their joining the Defence Force but were subject to automatic renewal when the period of full-time service ended. Defence Force units were given designations which reflected, and indeed in the majority of cases duplicated, the titles of the Territorial units whose drill halls they occupied.

The 1st (Defence Force) Battalion The Hertfordshire Regiment was raised on 9 April 1921 and was based on Hertfordshire Regiment drill halls. After serving the statutory period, the battalion was disbanded during July.


## 7.4  The National Defence Companies 1936–1939

The National Defence Companies, Territorial Army, were formed in September 1936 to undertake the Home Defence role once performed by the Royal Defence Corps. Since the Royal Defence Corps had been formed from the Supernumerary Companies, Territorial Force, which in turn had been raised from the National Reserve (see above), the National Defence Companies could reasonably be said to be the descendants of the National Reserve and, indeed, they were in many respects very similar. Their role was 'to protect important points in Great Britain (as far as possible in the neighbourhood of their own homes) on the threat of, and during, war'. They were not to be called up until it was necessary for guard forces to be deployed and meanwhile would be enrolled in peace-time 'as willing to be commissioned or enlisted for service in the local National Defence Company, if and when required'. Membership was restricted to former officers and men of H.M. Forces, providing that they had no reserve liability, and the minimum age for enrolment was forty-five years. It was envisaged that some 8500 officers and men would be enrolled throughout the country, any excess of volunteers being held on a waiting list. Uniforms and equipment would be issued only after actual commissioning or enlistment.

Each National Defence Company was affiliated to a local Territorial infantry battalion and administrative arrangements were handled by County Territorial Associations. Once enrolled, National Defence Company personnel were permitted to attend parades of their affiliated unit and to join its social clubs. The companies were organised in numbered groups on embodiment in August 1939 but the group system proved unsatisfactory and in November 1939 each group was converted into one or more Home Defence battalions of a Regular regiment of infantry of the line.[11]

A National Defence Company enrolled and administered by Hertfordshire Territorial Association was affiliated to 1st Battalion The Hertfordshire Regiment. Its establishment on embodiment was two hundred and fifty all ranks (the approximate equivalent of two infantry companies) but it is not clear whether it was fully recruited. The National Defence Companies affiliated to the 1st Battalion The Hertfordshire Regiment and the 5th Battalion The Bedfordshire and Hertfordshire Regiment together formed No. 6 Group, National Defence Companies, which was deployed to guard airfields in Bedfordshire, Hertfordshire and Cambridgeshire.

No. 6 Group was incorporated into the Bedfordshire and Hertfordshire Regiment as 7th (Home Defence) Battalion in November 1939 and the direct connection of National Defence Company personnel with the Hertfordshire Regiment was lost.

## 7.5   The Home Guard 1940–1945

The Home Guard sprang suddenly into being following a broadcast appeal by the Secretary of State for War on 14 May 1940. Initially the force was known as the Local Defence Volunteers and its formation was authorised by the Defence (Local Defence Volunteers) Regulations passed on 19 May. A further regulation ordered the change of title to Home Guard on 31 July 1940. Early in August authority was given for Home Guard battalions to become affiliated to their local Territorial battalions and to wear their cap badges. Initially the only other badge was an armlet with the letters 'L.D.V.' (later Home Guard). Eventually 'Home Guard' shoulder titles were issued, together with cloth patches designating the county and the battalion number.

For nearly a year, though recognised as part of the Armed Forces of the Crown, the Home Guard had to make do (as had the Volunteer Training Corps – see above) with 'appointed' rather than commissioned officers, and the use of military ranks was forbidden. (The agreed titles and badges of rank were published in August 1940.[12]) From February 1941 officers were commissioned and the normal army ranks were used, except that privates were styled 'Volunteer' – a rank dropped in favour of 'Private' when powers were taken in 1942 to direct enrolment into the Home Guard.

The basic Home Guard unit was the 'general service battalion' and the development of specialised or mobile units was closely controlled. However, substantial use was made of Home Guard anti-aircraft units and Home Guard detachments supplemented the Regular coast artillery. Home Guard motor transport companies – equivalent to the Royal Army Service Corps – were authorised in 1943. No matter what specialist role a Home Guard unit had, it always wore the cap badge of its affiliated infantry regiment.

'Stand Down' was ordered from 1 November 1944 and on Sunday 3 December final parades were held throughout the country. After nearly five years of valuable service, during which armament progressed from shot guns and cudgels to Sten guns, medium machine-guns and light artillery, and the overall strength reached nearly 1100 infantry battalions, with anti-aircraft batteries and supporting units of various types, the Home Guard was disbanded on 31 December 1945.

The original scheme for the raising of the Local Defence Volunteers in May 1940 provided for 'Hertfordshire Zone' to consist of one battalion with twenty companies based in the principal urban and rural areas. Nineteen companies were in fact raised – the designation 20 Company was originally allocated to zone headquarters company, which was not formed – and by July 1940 many companies had grown to a strength of over five hundred. The organisation was then rationalised by regrouping the companies geographically into seven battalions and forming new companies by division of the original ones. In September 1940 the 6th Battalion at Watford, which had become very unwieldy, was split to form the 8th, 9th and 10th Battalions. By the close of 1940 the ten battalions comprised thirty-five individually numbered companies. The ten-battalion organisation continued until July 1942, but there were some transfers of

Figure 7.6  *Hertfordshire Home Guard – An 'orders group' at Hitchin, October 1940. There has by now been a partial issue of the minimal uniform first authorised for the Home Guard – denim overalls, field service cap and 'Home Guard' brassard. The officer in uniform with papers (second from right) is wearing the bronze finish Hertfordshire Regiment cap badge in his field service cap. Two different rifles are in use, the .303-in. No. 3 Lee-Enfield and the .300-in. United States – manufactured P. 17.*
(Hitchin Museum)

Figure 7.7  *Hertfordshire Home Guard – Members of a Watford company taking a close look at a tank, August 1941. Battledress has now been issued and the white-on-khaki 'Home Guard' shoulder title is beginning to replace the brassard. The Hertfordshire Regiment cap badge can be clearly seen.*
(Watford Library)

Figure 7.8  *Hertfordshire Home Guard – Small arms training with the Thompson sub-machine gun and the Browning Automatic Rifle (on table), March 1942. These members of the 9th Battalion are wearing the county designation 'HTS' and the battalion numeral beneath the 'Home Guard' shoulder title – a practice which continued until Stand-Down.*
(© Fox Photos Ltd.)

companies between battalions and a further nine companies were raised, the last being 44 Company. Sweeping changes in organisation took place between July and September 1942, when five additional battalions were formed. At the same time the numbered companies lost their individual designations and companies were lettered within their battalions in the conventional way. They were, however, always referred to as, for example, '7B Company', rather than 'B Company, 7th Battalion'.

Late in December 1940, after several false starts, the designations of the Hertfordshire battalions were finally agreed. They had earlier been styled according to convention – for example the 1st Battalion Hertfordshire Home Guard – and for a few days in December they were known as the County of Hertford Home Guard. The new designation, which lasted until stand-down, was, for example, 1st Hertfordshire Battalion, Home Guard.

Hertfordshire Zone was sub-divided into two groups in March 1941 – No. 1 Group consisting of 6th, 7th, 8th, 9th and 10th Battalions and No. 2 Group consisting of 1st, 2nd, 3rd, 4th and 5th Battalions. Hertfordshire Zone was redesignated Hertfordshire Sub-Area in February 1942 and Nos. 1 and 2 Groups became Western and Eastern Groups respectively. The reorganisation and redesignation of July–September 1942 were completed on 1 October 1942, when Hertfordshire Sub-Area was reorganised, and at the same time redesignated Hertfordshire Sub-District. The Eastern Group was split in two to form Eastern Group (1st, 3rd, 11th and 12th Battalions) and Central Group (2nd, 4th, 5th, 13th, 14th and 15th Battalions). Western Group (7th, 8th, 9th and 10th Battalions) lost 6th Battalion to London District on re-alignment of district boundaries. Apart from the redesignation of groups as 'sectors' in February 1943, there were no further significant changes between October 1942 and stand-down. (It should be noted that some parts of south and east Hertfordshire which fell within the London District boundary – Bushey, Barnet, Cheshunt and Waltham Cross – were included in the recruiting area of the Middlesex Home Guard.)

Group (later sector) mobile reserve companies were formed with platoons drawn from each battalion in the group, and, as supplies of equipment increased, several battalions formed mobile companies. These typically consisted of three mobile rifle platoons on bicycles and a support platoon with anti-tank, medium machine-gun and light artillery (usually spigot mortar) sections, mounted in impressed civilian transport. The battalions had no headquarter companies, their duties being undertaken by one of the rifle companies, usually with an increased establishment. Each rifle company had integral signals, intelligence and medical platoons and frequently a spigot mortar platoon. Rifle platoons were equipped with rifles (normally the United States ·300 in. 'P.17'), sub-machine guns (the United States ·45 in. Thompson; later the ·9 mm Sten) and light automatic weapons (United States ·300 in. Browning or ·300 in. Lewis), much as in the Regular forces.

In addition to the fifteen general service battalions, further specialist units were raised in Hertfordshire. These included four light anti-aircraft troops which were deployed for the close air defence of the De Havilland factories at Hatfield (two troops) and Leavesden, the Handley-Page factory at Radlett and a motor transport company – 2004 Motor Transport Company – raised at St. Albans, with outlying platoons at Watford and Letchworth and forming part of East Central District Motor Transport Column. Public utilities like the G.P.O., London Transport and the railway companies formed their own Home Guard units. In many cases these

TABLE 7.2  *Home Guard – Hertfordshire Sub-District – March 1944*

SUB-DISTRICT H.Q. HERTFORD

*Eastern Sector*
Sector H.Q.:    Woolmer Green        Mobile Reserve Company:    Great Amwell

| *1st Hertfordshire Battalion* | *3rd Hertfordshire Battalion* | *11th Hertfordshire Battalion* | *12th Hertfordshire Battalion* |
|---|---|---|---|
| Bn. H.Q.: Much Hadham | Bn. H.Q.: Hertford | Bn.H.Q.: Bishop's Stortford | Bn.H.Q.: Letchworth |
| *Companies:* | | | |
| A  Buntingford | A  Hertford | A  Bishop's Stortford | A ⎫ |
| B  Little Hadham | B  Hertford | B  Bishop's Stortford | B ⎬ Letchworth |
| C  Ware | C  Hoddesdon | C  Sawbridgeworth | C ⎭ |
| F  Royston | D  Haileybury | D  Bishop's Stortford | D |
| | E  Hertford | | E  Baldock |

*Central Sector*
Sector H.Q.:    Harpenden        Mobile Reserve Company:    St. Albans

| *2nd Hertfordshire Battalion* | *4th Hertfordshire Battalion* | *5th Hertfordshire Battalion* | |
|---|---|---|---|
| Bn.H.Q.: King's Walden | Bn.H.Q.: Welwyn | Bn.H.Q.: Harpenden | |
| *Companies:* | | | |
| A  Hitchin | A ⎫ | A  Harpenden | |
| B  Hitchin | B ⎬ Welwyn Garden City | B  Wheathamstead | |
| C  Stevenage | C ⎭ | C  Redbourn | |
| | D  Welwyn | D  Harpenden | |
| | E  Welwyn Garden City | | |

| *13th Hertfordshire Battalion* | *14th Hertfordshire Battalion* | *15th Hertfordshire Battalion* | *Light Anti-Aircraft Troops* |
|---|---|---|---|
| Bn.H.Q.: Hatfield | Bn.H.Q.: Hatfield | Bn.H.Q.: St. Albans | |
| *Companies:* | | | |
| A ⎫ | A  Hatfield | A ⎫ | 13A  Hatfield |
| B ⎬ De Havilland's, | B  Jack Olding's | B ⎪ | 13B  Leavesden |
| C ⎬ Hatfield | C  Essendon | C ⎬ St. Albans | 13C  Hatfield |
| D ⎭ | D  Brookmans Park | D ⎪ | |
| E  Leavesden | | E ⎭ | 15A  Radlett |

*Western Sector*
Sector H.Q.:    King's Langley        Mobile Reserve Company:    Watford

| *7th Hertfordshire Battalion* | *8th Hertfordshire Battalion* | *9th Hertfordshire Battalion* | *10th Hertfordshire Battalion* |
|---|---|---|---|
| Bn.H.Q.: Chipperfield | Bn.H.Q.: Croxley Green | Bn.H.Q.: Garston | Bn.H.Q.: Watford |
| *Companies:* | | | |
| A  Hemel Hempstead | A  Rickmansworth | A  Bricket Wood | A ⎫ |
| B  Berkhamsted | B  Croxley Green | B  Abbots Langley | B ⎪ |
| C  Tring | C  Watford | C  Watford | C ⎪ |
| D  Kings Langley | D  Chorleywood | D  Watford | D ⎬ Watford |
| E  Boxmoor | | E  Garston | E ⎪ |
| | | | F ⎪ |
| | | | G ⎪ |
| | | | H ⎭ |

*Hertfordshire Sub-District Troops*

2004 Motor Transport Company:  St. Albans
Weapon Training Schools:  Great Amwell; Tring
Camouflage School:  Tewin

would have been independent of local units on mobilisation but they were frequently attached for training and administrative purposes. Home Guard auxiliary bomb disposal units were attached to the 4th, 9th, 10th and 13th Battalions, weapon-training schools were established at Great Amwell and Tring, and a camouflage school was also established at Tewin. An outline order of battle for the Home Guard within Hertfordshire Sub-District in March 1944 is given in Table 7.2. The total strength of the units and sub-units shown was then just over 22 000, compared with a manpower ceiling of about 28 000.

When affiliations to Territorial regiments were authorised in August 1940 all seven Hertfordshire battalions were affiliated to the Hertfordshire Regiment, as were all battalions raised subsequently. Hertfordshire Regiment cap badges were issued in November 1940. Officers were permitted to wear the Hertfordshire Regiment pattern of coloured field-service cap. Each battalion wore, in addition to the printed 'Home Guard' shoulder title, a rectangular printed flash with the abbreviated county designation 'HTS' and a square printed flash with the battalion number.

## 7.6   The Home Guard 1952–1957

Towards the end of 1951 it was decided that the Home Guard should be re-formed. The necessary legislation, the Home Guard Act, 1951, was complete by early December 1951 and enrolment began in April 1952. The new Home Guard consisted of infantry battalions only. Distinction was drawn between 'effective' battalions, raised in areas where the threat of invasion appeared to be more acute, and 'cadre' battalions raised elsewhere. Effective battalions could be recruited up to a peace establishment of nine hundred all ranks, while cadre battalions had a peace establishment of only fifty. It was envisaged that all battalions would expand to some 1500 after mobilisation. Enlistment was for two years and the training liability was for fifteen hours every three months.

Recruiting for the force was generally poor and in November 1952 the unrealistic battalion establishments were revised and some effective battalions were reduced to cadre. The new peace-time recruiting ceilings were three hundred all ranks for effective battalions and one hundred all ranks for cadre battalions. The Home Guard was reduced to reserve establishment (key personnel only in each battalion) in December 1955 and eventually disbanded in 1957.

Ten Home Guard battalions were raised in Hertfordshire, which was divided into two sectors – Eastern Sector with 1st, 2nd, 3rd, 4th and 5th Battalions (all effective battalions) and Western Sector with 7th, 8th, 9th and 10th Battalions (all cadre battalions). As in the earlier Home Guard, one battalion (again designated 6th Battalion) came under command of London District and some parts of south and south-east Hertfordshire fell within the recruiting area of the Middlesex Home Guard. Locations for company headquarters were selected (see Table 7.3) and in many cases actual buildings were earmarked for use on mobilisation, but unless companies were able to find accommodation in drill halls or cadet huts all training was centralised at battalion headquarters. The 8th and 9th Battalions were linked under the designation 8th/9th Battalion in July 1953 to economise on permanent staff and accommodation but the link was broken on reduction to reserve establishment. Reduction of all battalions was completed by the end of February 1956, and final close-down by the end of July 1957.

The designation of the battalions differed from that used during the war and was, for example, '1st Hertfordshire Home Guard Battalion'. All battalions were affiliated to the Hertfordshire Regiment, Territorial Army

TABLE 7.3  *Hertfordshire Home Guard – June 1955: Battalion Headquarters and proposed locations of Company Headquarters on mobilisation*[1]

| Eastern Sector | 1st Battalion | 2nd Battalion | 3rd Battalion | 4th Battalion | 5th Battalion |
|---|---|---|---|---|---|
| Battalion Headquarters | Hitchin | Baldock | Welwyn | Hertford | Bishop's Stortford |
| A Company | Hitchin | Royston | Welwyn | Hertford | Nuthampstead |
| B Company | Offley | Baldock | Welwyn Garden City | Hoddesdon | Little Hadham |
| C Company | Codicote | Letchworth | Hatfield | Stapleford | Ware |
| D Company | Stevenage | Weston | Welham Green | Walkern | Bishop's Stortford |

| Western Sector | 7th Battalion | 8th Battalion[2] | 9th Battalion[3] | 10th Battalion |
|---|---|---|---|---|
| Battalion Headquarters | St. Albans | Croxley Green | Watford | Hemel Hempstead |
| A Company | St. Albans | Rickmansworth | Garston | Kings Langley |
| B Company | St. Albans | Sarratt | Watford | Berkhamsted |
| C Company | Harpenden | Croxley Green | Oxhey | Tring |
| D Company | – | – | Watford | Hemel Hempstead |

[1] 6th Battalion was within the London District boundary
[2] Left flank companies of 8th/9th Battalion July 1953 – December 1955
[3] Right flank companies of 8th/9th Battalion July 1953 – December 1955

and wore the regimental badge (without the 1st Battalion's scarlet cloth backing) in the beret and red and white 'Hertfordshire' shoulder titles on the battledress blouse. Subsidiary 'Home Guard' titles were also worn, together with battalion numerals.

## 7.7  The Home Service Force

The intention to form a force to supplement Regular and Territorial units in the guarding of vital installations in the United Kingdom in time of war was announced in Parliament in March 1982. Enabling legislation for the force, to be known as the 'Home Service Force', was already contained in the Reserve Forces Act, 1980, which specifically provides for the raising, within the Territorial Army, of a separate Home Service Force liable for call-out only for service within the United Kingdom (see page 7). The force is recruited from former members of the Regular and Volunteer Reserve Forces (not necessarily Army) who have completed at least two years' satisfactory service. As a result no basic training is required and the annual training liability can be reduced to the minimum which is judged sufficient to enable members to keep up the basic military skills involved (at present thirteen days). The individual scale of clothing and equipment is also lower than that issued to members of N.A.T.O. and General Reserve units of the Territorial Army.

While no actual line of descent can be traced, it will be seen that the Home Service Force is the logical successor to the National Defence Companies and their predecessors the National Reserve (see above). The important difference is that the Home Service Force exists and trains in peace-time and members do not simply enter into an engagement to serve on call-out. The minimum age limit (twenty years) is also considerably lower than that for the previous forces since it is no longer judged necessary to channel younger men exclusively into N.A.T.O. and General Reserve units but rather to make maximum use of those who have the required military training and experience but may not be willing to give up the time necessary for units with higher annual training commitment.

Four 'pilot' companies, designated Nos. 1 to 4 Companies, Home Service Force, Territorial Army, were formed in September 1982, each under the sponsorship of a General Reserve battalion, to enable the new scheme to be assessed over two years. In the summer of 1984 the trial was pronounced successful and the plan for the expansion of the Home Service Force within a manpower ceiling of five thousand all ranks organised in forty-seven companies was announced in September 1984. It was judged impossible for all these companies to be sponsored by General Reserve battalions (that is the Territorial units with the closest similarity of role on mobilisation), with the result that some are sponsored by N.A.T.O. units of the Territorial Army (not all infantry) and some by permanent military establishments. The majority of the companies were due to form by mid-1985 but a few will not come on to the establishment until 1990. It was decided not to continue the series of individual company numbers started during the trial and a new system was devised by which most companies take the designation of their sponsor unit and are lettered or numbered in sequence after existing sub-units.

One of the pilot companies, designated No. 3 Company, Home Service Force, was raised in East Anglia and sponsored by 6th (Volunteer) Battalion The Royal Anglian Regiment. Since company headquarters and all three platoons were based in 6th Battalion drill halls there was no representation in Hertfordshire at this stage. On the expansion of the Home Service Force No. 3 Company was disbanded and four new companies were raised, sponsored by both 5th and 6th (Volunteer) Battalions. No. 6 (Home Service Force) Company, 5th (Volunteer) Battalion has company headquarters and one platoon at Chelmsford and one platoon at Vange, both in Essex, and one platoon with No. 4 (Hertford-shire) Company at Hertford. The Hertford platoon, designated 17 Platoon, began to recruit in the spring of 1985. and lost no time in recruiting close to full establishment. Members of the platoon took part in the nationwide Home Defence Exercise 'Brave Defender' in September 1985 and have since settled down to regular training for their important role of guarding 'key points' in the event of mobilisation.

## 7.8   The Auxiliary Territorial Service 1938–1939

The Auxiliary Territorial Service was formed in September 1938[13] to provide a force, initially 20 000 strong, of women organised and trained to support the army on mobilisation. The responsibility for raising A.T.S. units was given to County Territorial Associations and although the A.T.S. did not achieve recognition as part of the Armed Forces of the Crown until after mobilisation in 1939, it was for all practical purposes part of the Territorial Army. Each A.T.S. company was affiliated to a Territorial unit, which was tasked with providing elementary training in some military subjects, and many companies went to camp with their affiliated units in 1939. Companies were intended for employment in clerical duties, motor transport driving or 'general service' (that is with a mixed establishment of clerks, cooks, storewomen and orderlies) and in peace-time were either on higher establishment (fifty-six all ranks) or lower establishment (twenty-four all ranks). The A.T.S. was extensively reorganised after mobilisation and expanded to a maximum strength of 210 000 in 1943. Its duties were taken over by the Women's Royal Army Corps, raised in both the Regular and Territorial Armies, in 1949.

Hertfordshire raised four companies as part of the Bedfordshire and Hertfordshire Unit, A.T.S. All four were for general service. Two – 2nd and 3rd Hertfordshire Companies, at Watford and St. Albans respectively – were on higher establishment, while 13th and 14th Hertfordshire Companies, at Hitchin and Hertford, were on lower establishment. Both 3rd and 14th Companies were affiliated to the Hertfordshire Regiment. Members of the two companies went to camp with the regiment in 1939 and gave invaluable 'behind the scenes' assistance at this key period of the split into 'original' and 'duplicate' units (see page 74). The link between the A.T.S. and the regiment was, to the regret of both sides, severed shortly after mobilisation.

## 7.9 The Cadet Forces

Prior to the formation of the Territorial Force in 1908 authority existed for two types of cadet unit, or 'corps', raised under the provisions of *Regulations for the Volunteer Force*. Cadet companies forming part of Volunteer units were authorised as early as 1863, while independent cadet units were not introduced until 1886. Volunteer units lost their attached cadet corps on transfer to the Territorial Force. All those cadet units raised in schools (in fact the great majority) were offered the chance of joining the Junior Division of the newly-formed Officers Training Corps.[14] Independent units and the relatively few school units that did not opt to join the Officers Training Corps could apply, through their local Territorial Force Association, for War Office recognition, and Associations were specifically empowered to establish or assist cadet battalions or corps. The huge growth in the cadet movement that occurred during the First World War was almost entirely through Association sponsorship, rather than by additions to the Officers Training Corps. The expansion was further assisted by the raising of cadet corps affiliated to units of the Volunteer Force (see page 123).

The down-turn in interest in cadet units which followed the end of the First World War was further accelerated in 1930 by the withdrawal of all forms of official assistance to units raised under the auspices of County Associations. The Officers Training Corps was not affected by these measures, which proved the final blow to many cadet corps; those that survived were almost always in schools or institutions. A limited degree of official support was restored in December 1931, when the system of War Office recognition was resumed and units were again granted the privilege of wearing the badges of affiliated Territorial units, but no financial support was forthcoming.

On the outbreak of war in 1939 there was renewed interest in military training but few new army cadet units were raised, since the government directed that priority should be given to the formation of Air Training

Figure 7.9   *Haileybury College Cadet Corps – The shooting eight in 1887. The cadet-lieutenant (seated, centre) and cadets are wearing the uniform of the 1st Hertfordshire Rifle Volunteer Corps (compare with Figures 3.20 and 3.24) with the shoulder designation 1-C-HTF. Their shakos, with bugle badge, are probably an optional item of uniform worn only on the range (compare with Figures 3.6 and 3.21).*

(Haileybury College)

Figure 7.10   *Berkhamsted School Cadet Corps – The school contingent at the Royal Review of cadets at Windsor in 1897. Their grey uniform is modelled on that of the 2nd (Hertfordshire) Battalion The Bedfordshire Regiment, to which the corps was attached. Helmet plates, both for officers (extreme right) and cadets are identical to those shown in Figure 3.12.*

(Berkhamsted School)

Figure 7.11 (Left)   *Haileybury College Cadet Corps – The officers of the corps in undress, field day order, 1900. The uniform is obviously similar to that of the 1st (Hertfordshire) Volunteer Battalion The Bedfordshire Regiment (compare with Figure 3.31). Two different badges are being worn in the blue field service cap – one shown in Figure 3.18 (Right), the other evidently the same as their collar badge.*                                          (J. D. Sainsbury)

(Right)   *Berkhamsted School Cadet Corps – An officer in undress with helmet, 1901. Though best described as 'undress', his tunic with pockets may have been the only uniform then worn by the officers of the corps, the headgear and accoutrements being varied according to the occasion. The helmet plate is as shown in Figure 3.12 (Left) and the pouch belt badge as in Figure 3.13.*

(Berkhamsted School)

Figure 7.12   *Haileybury College Cadet Corps – Cadet non-commissioned officers with the permanent staff sergeant-major (seated, far right), 1901. They are wearing the undress scarlet uniform of the 1st (Hertfordshire) Volunteer Battalion The Bedfordshire Regiment (compare with Figure 3.30) with the designation 1-C-BEDFORD on the shoulder strap.*                    (Haileybury College)

[137]

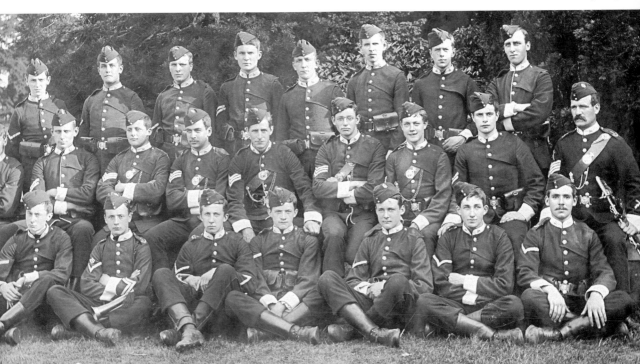

Figure 7.13   *Berkhamsted School Cadet Corps – Members assembling in the school grounds prior to a field day, or possibly the march to camp, c. 1907. The undress uniform is similar to that worn by the 2nd (Hertfordshire) Volunteer Battalion The Bedfordshire Regiment, with the badge shown in Figure 3.14. (Centre) worn on the turn-up of the slouch hat. The Martini-action rifles clearly visible in Figure 7.10 have been replaced by bolt-action Enfield rifles.*

(Berkhamsted School)

Corps units. The expansion of the Cadet Force, as it had become known, was announced in January 1942 and began in March the same year under the control of Cadet Committees of County Associations. Shortly afterwards the title of the Force was changed to Army Cadet Force.[15] Newly raised Army Cadet Force units were advised to become affiliated to local Home Guard battalions in order to take advantage of training facilities, but they were also required to become affiliated to local Territorial units, whose uniform and badges they were authorised to adopt, with the approval of the honorary colonel or commanding officer of the unit concerned. The organisation and administration of the Army Cadet Force under Cadet Committees of Territorial and Auxiliary Forces Associations has been changed relatively little up to the present time.

Soon after the outbreak of war in 1939, following the announcement that all candidates for commissions in H.M. Forces would have to serve a minimum period in the ranks, appointment direct to commissions from the Officers Training Corps ceased. The title of the Corps was accordingly changed in September 1940, the Senior Division becoming the Senior Training Corps and the Junior Division the Junior Training Corps.[16] In April 1948 Junior Training Corps contingents became part of the Combined Cadet Force and schools with Army Cadet Force units were invited, but not required, to transfer these units to the Combined Cadet Force.[17] The Combined Cadet Force continues at the present time as the more usual form of cadet unit in schools.

The Volunteer Force units in Hertfordshire had no attached cadet companies until 1886, when Haileybury College formed a cadet company attached to the 1st (Hertfordshire) Volunteer Battalion The Bedfordshire Regiment. Four more school cadet corps were raised between 1891 and 1906 and attached to appropriate battalions, but no units were formed outside schools. The five school corps transferred to the Junior Division, Officers Training Corps in July 1908. The first cadet company to be raised in Hertfordshire under the Territorial and Reserve Forces Act was officially recognised in April 1911. Four independent cadet companies and two Church Lads' Brigade battalions had been raised by the outbreak of war in 1914. A further ten cadet units were raised during the war, some of them consisting of more than one company, and one in 1920. The 8th Hertfordshire Cadets (St. Edmund's College) transferred to the Officers Training Corps in 1924 and only two units, the 9th Hertfordshire Cadets

Figure 7.14 *Berkhamsted School Officers Training Corps – Signals training, 1922. The cadets are wearing orthodox khaki service dress and are now the only users of the badge shown in Figure 3.14 (Centre), which is worn as a cap badge.*

(Berkhamsted School)

Figure 7.15 *St. Albans School Officers Training Corps – Camp guard, 1922. Cadets (three files to right) are wearing orthodox khaki service dress, while cadet non-commissioned officers (Left) have a uniform with strong similarities to officers' service dress. All ranks are wearing the cap badge of the Hertfordshire Regiment.*

(J. D. Sainsbury)

Figure 7.16 *7th Hertfordshire (Hitchin) Company, Army Cadet Force – Colonel E. C. M. Phillips, C.B., D.S.O., T.D., inspecting the company at Hitchin Grammar School, July 1943. The cadets are wearing the cap badge of the Hertfordshire Regiment (invisible in most cases owing to the angle of their caps) and the slip-on shoulder title shown in Figure 5.8 above an additional 'Cadet Force' title.*

(Hitchin Museum)

[139]

Figure 7.17 *St. Albans School Junior Training Corps – Signals training, 1947. The cap badge of the Hertfordshire Regiment can be seen in the khaki 'cap, general service' worn by the cadets.*

(St. Albans School)

Figure 7.18 *1st Cadet Battalion The Hertfordshire Regiment – Members of the battalion corps of drums with the regimental sergeant-major instructor of Hertford Grammar School Combined Cadet Force, 1950. The cadets are wearing the cap badge of the Hertfordshire Regiment, the sleeve badge shown in Figure 7.20 and the white-on-red embroidered shoulder titles 'Hertfordshire' and 'A.C.F'.*

(J. D. Sainsbury)

Figure 7.19 *Berkhamsted School Combined Cadet Force – Her Majesty Queen Elizabeth The Queen Mother inspects a Guard of Honour during her visit to the school in June 1956. Blue berets came into general use in cadet units in the early 1950s but neither cadets nor the Home Guard wore the red patch behind the Hertfordshire Regiment cap badge – a privilege reserved to the 1st Battalion and commemorating the red 'Ace of Hearts' patch worn during the First World War.*

(Berkhamsted School)

and the Royal Masonic School Cadet Corps (11th Hertfordshire Cadets) survived to be absorbed into the Army Cadet Force in 1942, with the Bishop's Stortford College Cadet Corps (12th Hertfordshire Cadets), raised in 1938.

On the expansion of the Army Cadet Force in 1942, a large number of cadet companies were raised in towns, villages and schools throughout the county. It is likely that there were about twenty-five companies but no complete list survives. Companies were numbered and each incorporated a local or school designation in its title, for example, 6th Hertfordshire (Letchworth Grammar School) Company, A.C.F. and 7th Hertfordshire (Hitchin) Company, A.C.F. In 1944 the independent numbered companies of the Army Cadet Force in Hertfordshire were grouped into eight battalions and their company numbers discarded in favour of the conventional letters.

Black printed 'Cadet Force' shoulder titles were worn with the embroidered slip-on title and cap badge of the Hertfordshire Regiment. Companies also wore the battalion numerals of the Home Guard battalions to which they were affiliated. At the stand-down of the Home Guard battalion numerals were replaced by a triangular county flash (see Figure 7.20). Cadet battalions affiliated to the Hertfordshire Regiment were authorised to wear embroidered white-on-red 'Hertfordshire A.C.F.' shoulder titles in January 1948.

The fact of the post-war run-down was recognised in February 1948 by a reorganisation which reduced the number of battalions from eight to four, two of which were affiliated to the Hertfordshire Regiment as the 1st and 4th Cadet Battalions. In 1952 a further reorganisation took place with the aim of forming one battalion – 1st Cadet Battalion The Hertfordshire Regiment – consisting of all detachments to the east of the Great North Road, with headquarters at Hertford, and one regiment – 4th Cadet Regiment (Hertfordshire Yeomanry) R.A. – consisting of all detachments to the west of the Great North Road, with headquarters at St. Albans. The Royal Masonic School battalion was unchanged. Certain adjustments to this layout were made subsequently, chiefly to incorporate the Welwyn Garden City detachment in the 4th Cadet Regiment and those at Hitchin,

Figure 7.20 *Hertfordshire Army Cadet Force – Embroidered sleeve badge, gold hart surrounded by red line on dark blue background, introduced shortly after the Second World War.*
(J. D. Sainsbury)

Letchworth and Baldock in the 1st Battalion. In 1961, following the changes in title of their parent units, the cadet units became 1st Cadet Battalion The Bedfordshire and Hertfordshire Regiment and 4th Cadet Regiment (Hertfordshire and Bedfordshire Yeomanry) R.A. Between 1952 and 1967 individual detachments of the A.C.F. were affiliated for training purposes to their nearest Territorial Army unit and wore the badges and titles appropriate to that unit. This arrangement gave rise to more than one cap badge and shoulder title within each cadet battalion or regiment.

There was no immediate requirement for changes in affiliation or badges when Territorial units were transferred to the Territorial and Army Volunteer Reserve in 1967, but with the reduction to cadre and eventual disbandment of the Bedfordshire and Hertfordshire Regiment (Territorial) in 1969–71 it became necessary for their cadets (both C.C.F. and A.C.F.) to link directly with the Royal Anglian Regiment. The 1st Cadet Battalion The Bedfordshire and Hertfordshire Regiment was therefore designated 1st (Hertfordshire) Cadet Battalion The Royal Anglian Regiment and rebadged accordingly.

The former 9th Hertfordshire Cadets, which had continued into 1st (Hertfordshire) Cadet Battalion as No. 1 Company, were disbanded in 1976 and the 11th Hertfordshire Cadets (Royal Masonic School), which had always been affiliated to the London Rifle Brigade (later Royal Greenjackets) were disbanded under the title 1st Cadet Battalion The London Rifle Brigade in 1977. All existing A.C.F. units and sub-units in Hertfordshire thus spring from the expansion of the A.C.F. in 1942 or are of more recent origin. Of the five present day Combined Cadet Force contingents, three (Haileybury, Berkhamsted School and St. Albans School) were raised as cadet companies attached to Volunteer battalions, one (Aldenham School) was raised directly in the Officers Training Corps in 1908; and one (St. Edmund's College, Ware) was re-raised in the Combined Cadet Force in September 1976, after a break in service of the contingent, originally 8th Hertfordshire Cadets, since January 1968.

The Hertfordshire cadet units at present affiliated to the Royal Anglian Regiment and thus carrying on the tradition of affiliation to Hertfordshire's Volunteer infantry are:

*Combined Cadet Force*
Haileybury, Berkhamsted School, Aldenham School, St. Edmund's College.

*Army Cadet Force*
1st (Hertfordshire) Cadet Battalion The Royal Anglian Regiment

Detachments: Hertford, Ware, Hoddesdon, Waltham Cross, Bishop's Stortford, Royston, Hitchin, Letchworth, Stevenage, Buntingford.

NOTES

1. A.O. 142/1910
2. A.O. 240/1911
3. A.O. 324/1911
4. A.O. 143/1913
5. A.C.I. 195/October 1914; A.O. 187/1915
6. A.C.I. 28/November 1915
7. A.C.I. 302/November 1915
8. A.O. 115/1916; A.C.I. 841/ April 1916
9. A.O. 7/1922
10. A.O. 208/1918
11. A.C.I. 742/1939
12. A.C.I. 924/1940
13. A.O. 199/1938
14. A.O.s 72 and 160/1908
15. A.O. 52/1942
16. A.O. 164/1940
17. A.O. 139/1948

# Chapter 8

# *Two Units not to be confused with the Hertfordshire Regiment*

## 8.1   The 49th (Hertfordshire) Regiment of Foot 1743–1881

Authority for the raising of the regiment that was eventually to carry the 'Hertfordshire' title was granted to Colonel Edward Trelawny, Governor of Jamaica, in June 1744. Communications with the island were such that although the authority was backdated to December 1743, the regiment was not actually mustered until early in 1745. It was formed from independent companies then garrisoning the island. Originally the regiment occupied sixty-third place in precedence, as shown by the *Army List*, but in 1748 it was moved into forty-ninth place following the disbandment of the 6th Regiment of Marines. The use of the Colonel's name to describe the regiment was discontinued in 1751 and thereafter it was known, following the precedence, as the 49th Regiment of Foot.

The regiment acquired its 'Hertfordshire' title when all numbered regiments received county designations in 1782. PETRE (see Bibliography) records that the regiment had no connection with the county but in a short article on the 49th Foot which appeared in *Hertfordshire Countryside*, BUSBY suggests that the then Colonel, the Hon. Alexander Maitland, of Totteridge, may have recommended the link with his own county. In 1816 the regiment was honoured with the additional title 'Princess Charlotte of Wales's'.

The single-battalion 49th Foot was linked with the 66th (Berkshire) Regiment of Foot, forming Sub-District 41, in 1873. The Sub-District Depot was established at Reading. (There had not previously been a depot in Hertfordshire; depot companies served in various stations in the United Kingdom as convenience dictated.) The link with Berkshire was confirmed at the expense of Hertfordshire in 1881, when the 49th and 66th Regiments became respectively the 1st and 2nd Battalions of Princess Charlotte of Wales's (The Berkshire Regiment), later the Royal Berkshire Regiment. On losing its own Regular infantry regiment Hertfordshire became part of the 16th Regimental District (see page 24). At no time were units of the Auxiliary Forces raised in Hertfordshire affiliated to the 49th Foot.

Although the regiment played an active part in various operations in the Caribbean and in the American War of Independence it appears not

Figure 8.1   *49th (Hertfordshire) Regiment of Foot – The 'China Dragon' awarded to the regiment with the battle honour 'China' in 1843. Authorised to be worn on 'Colours and appointments', the dragon featured prominently in the regiment's badges, and sometimes buttons, both before and after 1881. It is still worn as the centrepiece of the badge of the Duke of Edinburgh's Royal Regiment, surrounded by a coil of rope – an allusion to the 49th Foot's service on board H.M. Ships.*

to have been present at any action in sufficient numbers to be granted battle honours. This was due at least in part to the battalion's being split up and companies' being assigned to mixed formations, as for instance, on the unsuccessful expedition against Ostend in 1798, in which only the grenadier and light companies were included, grouped with other similar companies into grenadier and light battalions. The whole regiment took part in the campaign in North Holland in 1799 and saw service on board H. M. Ships at the Battle of Copenhagen in 1801. The regiment was already in Canada when war broke out against the United States in 1812 and it played a prominent part in operations along the frontier during the two-year campaign, including the action at Queenstown. After service in South Africa and India the regiment went to China in 1840 as part of the expeditionary force sent to carry out reprisals for the Chinese interference with the opium trade. Active operations lasted until the end of 1842 and on return to India in 1843 the 49th Foot was granted the honour of wearing the Chinese dragon on its Colours and appointments 'in consequence of its distinguished conduct and gallantry in China'.

The regiment's final active service before redesignation was in the Crimean War 1854–55, in which they gained three Victoria Crosses. It was after their service in the Crimea that the 49th Foot left the most tangible reminder of their association with the County of Hertfordshire, for in 1857 a fine stone memorial to more than four hundred officers and men who fell in action in the Crimea or died of sickness during the campaign was unveiled in All Saints' Church, Hertford. The Colours which the regiment had carried in the Crimea were laid up beside the memorial in 1862. Regrettably both the memorial and the Colours were destroyed in the fire which devastated All Saints' Church in December 1891. However, when the time came for a memorial to be erected in the church to the officers and men of the Hertfordshire Regiment who fell in the Great War 1914–1918 a design based on that of the original 49th Foot memorial was adopted. The battle honours awarded to the 49th Foot up to 1881 were:

'Egmont-op-Zee', 'Copenhagen'[1], 'Queenstown', 'China'[2], 'Alma', 'Inkerman', 'Sevastapol'.

In 1959 the Royal Berkshire Regiment (Princess Charlotte of Wales's) was amalgamated with the Wiltshire Regiment (Duke of Edinburgh's) to form the Duke of Edinburgh's Royal Regiment (Berkshire and Wiltshire). All these honours are now carried on the Regimental Colour of the new regiment.

## 8.2  The Hertfordshire Militia 1758–1919

Under the Militia Act, 1757, which marked the start of the Militia as a permanent force, the County of Hertfordshire was required to provide 560 officers and men towards the total of nearly 31 000 to be raised in England and Wales. Initial recruiting was swift and by December 1758 the new regiment was complete at its authorised strength. It was designated 'The Hertfordshire Militia' and is normally referred to as such in official documents. However, the unit itself preferred the spelling 'Hartfordshire' and this form of the title was frequently used, at least until 1881. The distinctive hart badge and sandy yellow (officially 'buff') facings were adopted at a very early stage in the regiment's history.

Embodied service followed quickly after formation and occupied a considerable part of the period between 1758 and the final fall of France in 1815, as the table below shows. After Waterloo Militia training took place only at irregular intervals and by the late 1840s the whole force, though legally still in existence, had fallen into decay, the Hertfordshire Militia following the nationwide trend.

TABLE 8.1  *Embodied Service of the Hertfordshire Militia 1759–1814*

| Period of embodiment | | Details of service |
|---|---|---|
| Seven Years' War | October 1759–<br>January 1763 | Garrison Duty:<br>South-East England |
| American War of<br>Independence | May 1778–<br>March 1783 | Garrison Duty:<br>South-East England |
| War with Revolutionary<br>France I | February 1793–<br>April 1802 | Garrison Duty:<br>South-East England |
| War with Revolutionary<br>France II | May 1803–<br>July 1814 | Garrison Duty:<br>May 1803–September 1811,<br>South-East England;<br>September 1811–June 1813,<br>Ireland; June 1813–July1814,<br>South-East England |

The Militia was extensively reorganised on the basis of voluntary enlistment in 1852 and a new Militia Act passed in June the same year. In August the Lord Lieutenant called for some 450 volunteers for the reconstituted Hertfordshire Militia and the new battalion did its first training in November. The following year Hatfield was recognised as the headquarters of the regiment. Office, store and armoury buildings were erected by the Marquess of Salisbury and rented by him to the county authorities, who were still responsible for providing the necessary accommodation for the Militia out of the county rates. The battalion was organised on a basis of eight companies and the establishment was finally fixed at thirty officers and 825 rank and file. In contrast to the Rifle Volunteer Corps (see Chapter Three) Militia companies were raised from the county as a whole and no attempt was made to affiliate them to particular towns.

The Hertfordshire Militia volunteered its services during the Crimean War and the battalion was embodied in December 1854. It did duty in the Aldershot Command, receiving new Colours while there, and was disembodied in June 1856. Militia battalions were frequently, even in Napoleonic times, encouraged to provide recruits for the Line from their ranks and during these two years' embodied service the Hertfordshire Militia provided five hundred recruits; seven officers were also granted Regular commissions. The Hertfordshire Militia was not among the regiments embodied during the Indian Mutiny. Regiments which were embodied during the Crimean War were not called out for annual training in 1857, but thereafter annual training took place regularly until the turn of the century.

Under the Sub-District Brigade scheme of 1873 the Hertfordshire Militia was attached to the 33rd Sub-District Brigade, whose brigade depot was Bedford. Also attached to the brigade were the Bedfordshire and Huntingtonshire Regiments of Militia, the 1st Administrative Battalion Bedfordshire Rifle Volunteers and the 1st and 2nd Administrative Battalions Hertfordshire Rifle Volunteers (see page 22). The association with the brigade seems to have been very loose and had practical significance only in the arrangements for recruit training.

Figure 8.2   *The Hertfordshire Militia – (Left) A captain in full dress, c. 1865. His scarlet tunic has buff facings on the collar, which also carries his badges of rank, and at the 'slash' cuffs. The hart 'trippant' regimental badge appears on his belt clasp but he is unmistakably Militia – the Volunteers, and then only the 1st Battalion, did not adopt scarlet until 1897. (Centre) A captain in full dress just before officers' badges of rank were moved from the collar to the shoulder cords in 1880. The pointed cuff replaced the 'slash' cuff in 1868. Again, though the hart 'trippant' can be distinguished on helmet plate and belt clasp, this officer is unmistakably Militia. (Right) A subaltern officer in undress braided patrol jacket, 1880. The hart badge on his forage cap is unlike any worn by the Hertfordshire Rifle Volunteers but should not be confused with similar badges worn by the Hertfordshire Constabulary.*                                                    (J. D. Sainsbury)

In 1881 the 33rd Sub-District Brigade was superseded by the 16th Regimental District, also with headquarters at Bedford. The Regular and Militia battalions of the brigade were redesignated, the Hertfordshire Militia being absorbed into the Bedfordshire Regiment as the 4th Battalion, but retaining the designation 'Hertfordshire Militia' in brackets.

The uniform of the Bedfordshire Regiment was laid down as 'Scarlet, facings white'. This necessitated changing the Hertfordshire Militia's buff facings, and in 1882 re-badging took place. All battalions of the Bedfordshire Regiment adopted a new headdress badge, in which the badge of the Hertfordshire Militia – a hart crossing a ford – displaced the numeral XVI, formerly worn by the 16th Foot, in the centre of the star of the Order of the Bath. The new collar badge was a hart 'trippant' and scroll inscribed 'Bedfordshire'. Apart from 'M' above the 'Bedford' shoulder title, the Militia battalions were dressed identically to the Regular battalions.

In January 1900 the 4th Battalion was embodied for garrison service in the United Kingdom but it quickly volunteered to go to South Africa and sailed in February, joining 9 Brigade on arrival. The battalion itself spent most of its service administering martial law in territories regained from the Boers but it found a company of mounted infantry which earned special distinction in action with Lord Methuen's column. Thirty-two non-commissioned officers and men lost their lives in South Africa and the

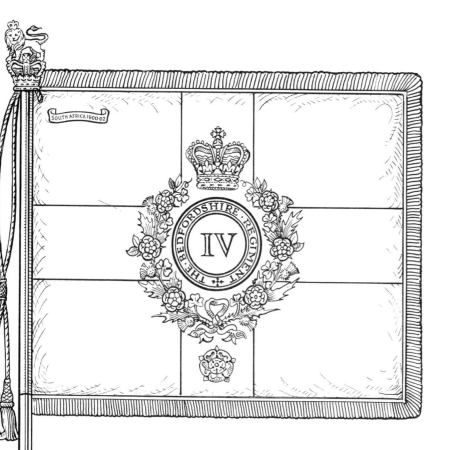

Figure 8.3 *4th Battalion The Bedfordshire Regiment (Hertfordshire Militia) – Regimental Colour presented in 1891 and laid up in St. Etheldreda's Church, Hatfield in 1920. The Colour conforms to the pattern laid down in 1881 for 'non-royal English regiments of infantry of the line. The Bedfordshire Regiment was not authorised to carry a badge in the centre of its Regimental Colour until 1934 (see pages 50–51 and compare with Colour Plate 1), as a result the battalion's number in Roman numerals appears in the centre. The battle honour scroll 'South Africa 1900–02' has been fixed in the wrong position; as a single honour it should appear on the lower arm of the St. George's Cross.*

(Drawing by Geoffrey Mussett)

battalion earned its first decorations for distinguished service and the battle honour 'South Africa 1900–'02'.

There was a further reform of the Militia under Lord Haldane. The Territorial and Reserve Forces Act, 1907, provided for the transfer of the Militia by Order in Council to the Army Reserve as units of the Special Reserve. Conditions of service remained substantially the same but the role on mobilisation was altered to one of finding reinforcement drafts for line battalions, rather than active service as units. The necessary Order in Council was passed on 9 April 1908, authorising the transfer of all Militia units to the Special Reserve after their annual training.

The 4th Battalion The Bedfordshire Regiment completed its annual training on 14 June 1908 and was transferred to the Special Reserve with effect from that date. It was described as an 'Extra Reserve' battalion, the 3rd Battalion (Bedfordshire Militia) being Special Reserve, but there was no difference in terms of service or other significant details.

On the outbreak of war in August 1914 the 4th Battalion was embodied and allotted to the fixed defences of the port of Harwich. Frequent drafts were sent to France but, as new arrangements for training reinforcements were introduced, it was decided to release certain Special Reserve battalions, among them the 4th Battalion, for service at the front. The battalion joined 190 Brigade of 63rd (Royal Naval) Division in France in July 1916. After several weeks of training 190 Brigade took over part of the line near Hamel, just north of the Ancre, in October, and joined in the closing stages of the Battle of the Somme and the first battle for the Beaumont Hamel Ridge in November 1916. For the next three months the battalion remained on the Ancre and took part in the advance up the valley in February 1917 which pushed the enemy back to the Hindenburg Line.

63rd Division then moved north in preparation for the Battle of Arras. In the opening stages of the battle in April 1917 the battalion led the successful attack on Gavrelle but was so reduced by casualties that for the subsequent attack on Oppy it was amalgamated with 7th Royal Fusiliers. After spending some time re-forming and training the 4th Battalion moved north again with 63rd Division to take part in the closing stages of the

Figure 8.4 (Left)   *The Hertfordshire Militia – A sergeant in full dress with the regimental mascot, 1880. The 1st Volunteer Battalion never wore the shako with scarlet full dress (see Figure 3.29). Additional indicators that this man is in the Militia are his sergeant's sash – sergeants in the Rifle Volunteers wore leather cross-belts – and the pointed cuff, which was not used by the Volunteers until 1907.*

(Right)   *4th Battalion The Bedfordshire Regiment (Hertfordshire Militia) – An officer in service dress, 1914. From the introduction of officers' khaki service dress in 1902 the officers of the 4th Battalion wore the hart trippant (actually a left-hand collar badge) as a cap badge. This practice persisted well into, if not throughout, the First World War and at first glance may lead to confusion with officers of the Hertfordshire Yeomanry. In fact, the Yeomanry officers' badge showed no title on the scroll, while that of the Militia was inscribed 'Bedfordshire'. The buttons were quite different, too, of course.*

(J. D. Sainsbury)

Third Battle of Ypres in October–November 1917, remaining on the Ypres front until the turn of the year.

The German spring offensive (21 March 1918) found 63rd Division near Marcoing on the Cambrai front. The enemy made little progress against the division but eventually circumstances forced its withdrawal. The 4th Battalion particularly distinguished itself in the rearguard action and in the counter-attack near Albert which finally halted the German advance in that sector. The commanding officer, Lieutenant-Colonel J.S. Collings-Wells, was posthumously awarded the Victoria Cross for sustained gallantry and leadership during this period. There followed some weeks in reserve, after which the battalion went into the line again near Achiet-le-Grand in May, and remained in that sector to take part in the Battle of Albert in August–September 1918. At the end of September the final allied offensive began with the attack on the Hindenburg Line. Advancing through Quéant, the battalion had a stiff fight on the banks of the Canal du Nord and reached the outskirts of Cambrai before being withdrawn to reserve. On 8 November the battalion rejoined the battle, now on the First Army front. It took part in the attack on Blaugies and by the cease-fire had reached Harmignies, south-east of Mons.

The 4th Battalion served in the Army of Occupation for several months before demobilisation. It had no corporate existence after demobilisation but it was not until 1953 that, in common with other Special Reserve units, it ceased to be shown in the *Army List*.

The early history of the Hertfordshire Militia may be found in Fellows and Hay. Some details of service in South Africa were included in *The Hart*, a regimental journal published in 1903 and 1904, and a record of service in the First World War appeared in *The Wasp* September 1927–December 1928, which should be read in conjunction with Jerrold.

NOTES

1. It was not until October 1951 that the Royal Berkshire Regiment was authorised to bear on their Regimental Colour the naval crown normally associated with battle honours awarded for service on board H.M. Ships.

2. With the dragon

Chapter 9

# How to find out more about The Hertfordshire Regiment

*Published works are referred to by their author, thus –* FORTESCUE *or by title in italics. Full details will be found in the Bibliography.*

## 9.1 Background to the Volunteer Force and the Territorial Army

The history of the Napoleonic volunteer associations is fully covered by SEBAG-MONTEFIORE and FORTESCUE who should be consulted in association with the *London Gazette* and the *Volunteer Army Lists* for the period, as well as the relevant Acts of Parliament (see Appendix 1) and Home Office papers in the Public Record Office (H.O. 51).

The period 1859–1908 has been considered in detail by CUNNINGHAM and BECKETT. A wealth of additional material is available in *Auxiliary and Reserve Forces Circulars, Army Orders*, the *London Gazette*, the *Monthly Army List* and *Volunteer Force Regulations*. There is no source in the Public Record Office equivalent to the collected papers in H.O. 51 but the serious student may wish to examine the reports of various Royal Commissions which considered the Militia, Yeomanry Cavalry and Volunteer Force during the period (traceable through the index to Command Papers). An invaluable background source is *The Times* newspaper (indexed).

The Territorial Force (later Territorial Army) has yet to be scrutinised in the manner of, for example, FORTESCUE or BECKETT. A great deal of material is available, however, in *Army Orders, Army Council Instructions*, the *Monthly Army List* and *Territorial Force/Territorial Army Regulations*. The *Territorial Year Book* gives a good nationwide survey but unfortunately the 1909 edition appears to have been the only one published; BAKER is similarly factual. First World War histories can be traced in outline through BECKE and JAMES and in detail in unit war diaries in the Public Record Office (W.O. 95). Unfortunately the official Order of Battle for the Second World War (JOSLEN) has nowhere near the degree of detail found in BECKE. Unit war diaries 1939–45 are now available in the Public Record Office subject to certain conditions. *The Times* remains a valuable guide to the history of the Territorial Army but should be read in conjunction with the published White Papers and *Soldier – The British Army Magazine* after 1947.

## 9.2 The Napoleonic Volunteers in Hertfordshire

The Muster Rolls for the Hertfordshire Volunteer Infantry 1804–1809 are in the Public Record Office (W. O. 13/4371–72). They should be examined in conjunction with the Home Office papers relating to the formation and disbandment of the Volunteer Infantry (H. O. 51). A few Muster Rolls covering the last year or so of the Hertfordshire Volunteer Infantry are in the Hertfordshire County Record Office, where there is also a substantial collection of papers relating to the Hitchin Volunteer Association (Hine/ Wilshere Papers) and a copy of the 'Stations of the Volunteers' map. Useful additional material on the Hitchin Volunteer Association is held at

Hitchin Museum. Items of uniform are at both Hitchin and Hertford Museums.

The account of the Royal Review at Hatfield by SALISBURY is important. The Review was also described in *The Times* and *The Gentleman's Magazine*. HINE has digested material from the Wilshere Papers in the County Record Office and BUSBY has also made extensive use of these papers. WILLSON's 'Chart' is in the principal museums and libraries and facsimile editions have been published. In addition, MOORE has examined the Muster Roll of the Hitchin Volunteer Association as evidence of the standard of literacy at the time and PIGRAM has also covered the Hitchin Volunteers. The BRIDGEMAN marches are in the British Library.

## 9.3   The Rifle Volunteers in Hertfordshire

The *Hertfordshire Almanac* provides a detailed directory of units and sub-units together with the appointments of officers and, frequently, senior non-commissioned officers. Local newspapers usually carried full accounts of Volunteer activities, notably annual training, dinners, balls, etc. Some badges and items of uniform are held at Hertford Museum and photographs are in the collections at Hitchin Museum, Hertford Museum, and Watford Public Library.

The later period (*c.* 1895–1905) and the participation of the active service companies in South Africa is covered by WROUGHTON and the 1st Volunteer Battalion's *Standing Orders*. Local newspapers published accounts of the departure and return of the various companies, 'letters from the Front' and accounts of parades at which medals were presented. Further details of individuals' service can be obtained from the Medal Rolls for the Queen's South Africa Medal in the Public Record Office (W.O. 100/176) and the 2nd Volunteer Battalion's Muster Book *c.* 1893–1908 in the County Record Office, which also contains a record of awards of the Queen's South Africa Medal to personnel of the battalion.

## 9.4   The Hertfordshire Regiment

The very early history of the regiment is contained in RICHARDS, with additional material on the Colours in *Hertfordshire Countryside*, Winter 1954–55 and June 1973. *Standing Orders* were published in 1911.

Coverage of the regiment in the *Hertfordshire Almanac* continues in detail until 1915, after which date officers only are listed and the *Monthly Army List* provides a better source. Local newspapers are useful both before and after mobilisation but the impact of censorship on security grounds increased as the war continued. The 1st/1st Battalion is mentioned from time to time in the Official History (EDMONDS), which is well indexed. (Reference should also be made to index entries for the brigades in which the battalion was serving.) There is no published history of 39th Division, with which the 1st/1st Battalion spent the greater part of their time in France, but the period up to February 1916 is covered by WYRALL. The most comprehensive sources for the battalion's First World War history are the War Diary 1914–1919, which is in the Public Record Office (W.O. 95), with transcripts in Hertfordshire County Record Office and the Imperial War Museum, and Gripper's collected notes for a regimental history in the County Record Office. Useful personal reminiscences can be found in CROFT and in *Hertfordshire Countryside,* May 1968 and September 1969. The names of those who died on active service are listed in the regiment's own *List of Officers, Warrant Officers, N.C.O.s and Other Ranks who were killed or died . . .,* a copy of which is in the County Record Office, and, with additional personal details in *Officers died . . .* and *Soldiers died . . .* Some routine orders of the two '2nd-Line', battalions are in the County Record Office and a memoir of service with the 4th/1st Battalion by F. T. H. Bennett is in the Imperial War Museum. Very few useful photographs of any of the First World War battalions seem to have survived.

Local newspapers and 'Battalion Notes' in *The Wasp* span the inter-war period. New *Standing Orders* were published in 1934. The expansion of the two battalions can be traced in the Longmore Papers at Hertford Museum, which are a useful background source, though in many cases duplicating the Hertfordshire Territorial and Auxiliary Forces Association's Minute Books – another essential record – in the County Record Office. A short series of photographs of 1938–39 is in Watford Public Library and others (from the *Hitchin Pictorial*) are in Hitchin Museum.

The history of both battalions during the Second World War is well covered by published material. 'C.F.D.' deals with the period 1939–1943 in outline. The 1st Battalion's tour in Italy is described in detail in the *Hertfordshire Field Gazette* and in articles by G. W. H. Peters in *The Wasp* September 1950 – June 1952 and *The Wasp and The Eagle,* June 1963 – June 1964. The *History of the First Division* (in the County Record Office) has numerous references to the 1st Battalion and excellent maps but is not indexed; ORGILL has occasional references. The principal publicly available contemporary sources are the battalion War Diaries 1939–1945 in the Public Record Office (W.O. 166, 170 and 176) and Overseas Service Diary 1943–1946 in the County Record Office. Service in Palestine is covered in 'Battalion Notes' in *The Wasp* 1945–46 and by WILSON. The 2nd Battalion's War Diaries are similarly in the Public Record Office (W.O. 166 and 171) and a useful account of the battalion's service in Normandy by J. R. HARPER appears in *The Wasp,* June 1945. Papers relating to claims by both battalions for battle honours for the Second World War are in the County Record Office but records of decorations and those who lost their lives are not yet readily available. Photographs of either battalion during this period are very scarce.

Three published sources give brief general histories of the Hertfordshire Regiment up to and including the re-formation of the 1st Battalion in 1947 – *A Short History . . ., The Territorial and Auxiliary Forces of Hertfordshire* and PETERS. Local newspapers, T. & A.F.A. papers and *The Wasp* remain useful sources for the period 1947–61, with the Presentation of Colours in 1953 covered by the Souvenir Programme illustrated in colour, copies of which are in the County Record Office and County Library. References to the regiment are to be found in *Hertfordshire Countryside,* notably Autumn 1946 and Autumn 1954.

## 9.5 Successor Units

The formation and early history of the 1st Battalion The Bedfordshire and Hertfordshire Regiment is dealt with in detail in *The Wasp and The Eagle,* December 1961 and June 1963, and 'Battalion Notes' appear in successive numbers. A typescript *Regimental History* was produced in 1963 and copies

have been quite widely deposited, as have copies of the illustrated
Souvenir Programme for the Presentation of New Colours to the battalion
in 1963. 'Battalion Notes' for the Volunteer battalions of the Royal Anglian
Regiment are in successive numbers of *The Castle* and all three battalions
are mentioned in BARTHORP.

# Appendix 1

*Principal Acts of Parliament authorising the raising and maintenance in England of Infantry units of the Auxiliary Military Forces, other than the Militia*

| | |
|---|---|
| **1794**<br>34 Geo.III c. 31 | Authorises the raising of volunteer forces during the present war. |
| **1798**<br>38 Geo.III c. 27 | *Defence of the Realm Act*<br>Authorises Volunteer Associations for local defence. |
| **1802**<br>42 Geo.III c. 66 | Authorises Volunteer Corps raised under the 1794 and 1798 Acts to continue during the Peace and new corps to be formed. |
| **1804**<br>44 Geo.III c. 54 | *Volunteer Consolidation Act*<br>Consolidates and amends earlier legislation. Authorises Volunteer Corps already in existence to continue and new Corps to be formed. |
| **1808**<br>48 Geo.III c. 111 | *Local Militia Act*<br>Authorises the formation of a permanent Local Militia liable for service throughout Great Britain and for call-out in aid of the Civil Power in their own and adjoining counties. Existing Volunteer Corps may transfer. |
| **1812**<br>52 Geo.III c. 38 | *Local Militia Act*<br>Revises earlier legislation. Provides for counties to be sub-divided for the purposes of providing Local Militia battalions. |
| **1863**<br>26 & 27 Vic. c. 65 | *Volunteer Act*<br>Permits Her Majesty to accept offers of service of Volunteer Corps and authorises corps accepted under earlier legislation to continue. Replaces Volunteer Consolidation Act, 1804 as enabling legislation for volunteer forces except the Yeomanry Cavalry. |
| **1871**<br>34 & 35 Vic. c. 86 | *Regulation of the Forces Act*<br>Removes control of local auxiliary forces from Lords Lieutenant, vesting it wholly in the Crown. |
| **1907**<br>7 Edw.VII c. 9 | *Territorial and Reserve Forces Act*<br>Formation of the Territorial Force and Special Reserve. Units of the Imperial Yeomanry and the Volunteer Force to be transferred to the Territorial Force and units of the Militia to the Special Reserve with effect from 1 April 1908. Volunteer Act, 1863 still available for the raising of volunteer forces in addition to the Territorial Force. |
| **1916**<br>6 & 7 Geo.V c. 62 | *Volunteer Act*<br>Authorises the acceptance of offers by individual members of Volunteer Corps to enter into agreements involving duties additional to those required under the Volunteer Act, 1863 for the duration of the present war. |

**1921**
11 & 12 Geo.V c. 37

*Territorial Army and Militia Act*
Territorial Force re-designated Territorial Army. Powers to raise or maintain any additional Auxiliary Forces (notably those conferred by the Volunteer Act, 1863 and the Militia and Yeomanry Act, 1901) cease.

**1939**
2 & 3 Geo.VI c. 62

*Emergency Powers (Defence) Act*
Enabling legislation for the Defence (Local Defence Volunteers) Regulations, 1940 (1940 No. 748) establishing the Local Defence Volunteers (later the Home Guard) for the period of the present emergency.

**1951**
15 & 16 Geo.VI c. 8

*Home Guard Act*
New, permanent authority for the raising of the Home Guard, the previous authority having lapsed on cessation of hostilities. Still in force.

**1953**
1 & 2 Eliz.II c. 50

*Auxiliary Forces Act*
Consolidates earlier legislation relating to the Territorial Army. Replaces the Territorial and Reserve Forces Act, 1907 as enabling legislation.

**1966**
c. 30

*Reserve Forces Act*
Territorial and Army Volunteer Reserve to be formed on 1 April 1967 by transfer of units of the Territorial Army and the Army Emergency Reserve. Provides for a specific force for Home Service.

**1980**
c. 9

*Reserve Forces Act*
Replaces the Reserve Forces Act, 1966 as the enabling legislation for the Territorial and Army Volunteer Reserve. Consolidates earlier legislation relating to the Reserve and Auxiliary Forces. Confirms provision for a separate force for Home Service.

**1982**
c. 14

*Reserve Forces Act*
Changes the title of the Territorial and Army Volunteer Reserve to 'Territorial Army'.

# Appendix 2

## *The Barnet Volunteers*

While the infantry volunteers raised at Barnet in Napoleonic times were firmly included amongst the Hertfordshire volunteer infantry in official lists and, for example, the map reproduced as Figure 2.6, the same did not hold good of infantry raised in the Barnet district after 1859. They looked across the county boundary to Middlesex and thus had no connection with the Hertfordshire Rifle Volunteers or, later, the Hertfordshire Regiment. The outline history below has been included in this work to complete, however briefly, the history of all infantry units raised in Hertfordshire and to direct readers with a particular interest in Barnet to alternative sources.

### Volunteer Force 1859–1908

A corps designated 12th Middlesex Rifle Volunteers was raised at Barnet in October 1859 and incorporated (with the 33rd, 35th and 41st Middlesex Rifle Volunteers) in the 6th Administrative Battalion, Middlesex Rifle Volunteers, in August the following year. As in Hertfordshire, the constituent corps of the Middlesex administrative battalions retained their original numbered designations – a feature which was, perhaps unusually, guaranteed by the notice of formation of the 6th Battalion published in the *London Gazette* of 7 September 1860. In January 1862 the 6th Administrative Battalion, which had by then lost the 35th Middlesex, was absorbed into the 2nd Administrative Battalion, which thereafter consisted of the 3rd Middlesex (Hampstead), 12th Middlesex (Barnet), 13th Middlesex (Hornsey), 14th Middlesex (Highgate), 33rd Middlesex (Tottenham) and 41st Middlesex (Enfield) Corps. Battalion headquarters was at Highgate until the mid-1870s when it moved to Hornsey. The six constituent corps of the 2nd Administrative Battalion were consolidated in 1880 to form the 3rd Middlesex Rifle Volunteer Corps. The consolidated corps became a Volunteer battalion of the Middlesex Regiment in 1881 and was accorded the status of 1st Volunteer Battalion. However, it retained the designation 3rd Middlesex Rifle Volunteer Corps until 1897, after which it was described in the *Army List* as '1st Volunteer Battalion (late 3rd Middlesex)'. The battalion contributed to the two volunteer active service companies, formed from all three Volunteer battalions, which were attached to the 2nd Battalion The Middlesex Regiment in South Africa and was awarded the battle honour 'South Africa, 1900–02'.

The 2nd Administrative Battalion adopted a grey uniform with scarlet facings which lasted for some thirty years, after which the colour of the facings was changed to grey. When the designation 1st Volunteer Battalion was adopted in 1897, the uniform was changed to scarlet with white facings.

### Territorial Force 1908–1919

The 1st Volunteer Battalion was transferred to the Territorial Force in 1908 to form the 7th Battalion The Middlesex Regiment – the senior Territorial battalion. (The Regiment then had four Regular and two Special Reserve battalions. Four Territorial battalions were formed, designated 7th – 10th). The 1st/7th Battalion and three battalions raised after mobilisation served during the First World War, as follows;

*1st/7th Battalion*
Original '1st-Line' unit. Mobilised in the Middlesex Infantry Brigade of the Home Counties Division. Left Home Counties Division and served September 1914 – February 1915 in Gibraltar Garrison. Joined 23 Infantry Brigade, 8th Division in   [157]

France March 1915 and served with the division until February 1916 without taking part in any major actions. Transferred to 167 Infantry Brigade, 56th (London) Division February 1916 and with the division took part in the Somme offensive, July–October 1916; the push to the Hindenburg Line, March–April 1917; the battles of Arras, April–May 1917, Ypres, August 1917 and Cambrai, November–December 1917; the blocking of the German spring offensive near Arras, March 1918; and the 'Advance to Victory', August–November 1918.

*2nd/7th Battalion*
Raised September 1914 as a '2nd-Line' battalion and incorporated in 201 Brigade, 67th (2nd Home Counties) Division. Left 67th Division February 1915 on embarkation for Gibraltar; served in Gibraltar Garrison February–August 1915; served in Egypt September 1915–May 1916 and took part in the campaign against the Sennusi on the Western Frontier. Disembarked in France mid-May 1916 and whole battalion placed in quarantine; disbanded in France mid-June 1916 and personnel largely absorbed into 1st/7th Battalion. (The 3rd/7th Battalion succeeded to the designation 2nd/7th – see below.)

*3rd/7th Battalion*
Raised February 1915 as an additional '2nd-Line' battalion and incorporated in 201 Brigade, 67th (2nd Home Counties) Division; became 2nd/7th Battalion on disbandment of original 2nd/7th (see above); served in 67th Division in Kent until disbanded early November 1917.

*4th/7th Battalion*
Raised May 1915 as a '3rd-Line' reception and training unit; redesignated 4th (Reserve) Battalion April 1916; absorbed 8th, 9th and 10th (Reserve) Battalions September 1916 and thereafter was the only Reserve Territorial battalion of the Middlesex Regiment; served as a draft-finding unit in Home Counties Reserve Brigade until disbanded in March 1919.

The Barnet company was not re-formed when the 7th Battalion took its place in the post-war Territorial Force (shortly to become the Territorial Army) in 1920 and Barnet has had no connection with Territorial infantry since.

The attempt to raise a Barnet-based battalion of the Volunteer Training Corps as part of the Hertfordshire Volunteer Regiment is described briefly in Chapter Seven, where it will also be seen that Barnet units of the Home Guard came under command of London District and wore the badges of the Middlesex Regiment.

# Appendix 3

## Extracts from the Monthly Army List

### 1. September 1879

#### Hertfordshire.
[51.]
(Sub-District No. 33.)
ADMINISTRATIVE BATTALIONS
1 A. Bn. *Little Gaddesden,*
*Great Berkhampstead.*

Comprising 2nd, 3rd, 4th, 5th
and 7th Corps.
*Major.*
James John Gape, *late* Maj.
Herts Mil., *p.*          13Mar.65
*Adjutant.*
Bevil Granville, *capt.*, *late* Bt.
Maj. 23 F.              4Oct.65
(*temp. Capt. in Army* 25Feb.74)
*Surgeon.*
Alfred Thos. Brett, *M.D.* 23Feb.61
*Hon. Chaplain.*
Rev. John W. Cobb      20Dec.71

[*Grey—facings Green.*]

---

#### 2 A. Bn. *Hertford.*
Comprising 1st, 6th, 9th, 10th and
14th Hertfordshire, and the 22nd
Essex Rifle Vol. Corps.
*Lieut. Colonel.*
The Earl Cowper, K.G.,
*p.s.*                  24Oct.60
*Majors.*
Wm. Leask, *p.*          8July74
Arthur M. Blake, *late* Lt. &
Capt. Gren. Gds., *p.* 27Nov.78
*Adjutant.*
Arthur Campbell-Walker,
*late* Capt. 79 F.       8Aug.77
                        14Jan.68
(*temp. Capt. in Army* 25Feb.74)
*Qua. Mast.*
John R. Cocks, *p.*      2Dec.74
*Surgeons.*
Geo. Elin, *M.D.*       22Jan.61
Daniel B. Balding      31May77
                        1Oct.77

[*Grey—facings Scarlet.*]

---

#### CORPS.

**1st.—*Hertford.* 2 A. Bn.**
*Capt. Commandant.* (1)
Augustus Hawks, *p.*     31Dec.70
*Captain.* (1)
Thos. J. Sworder, *p.*   31Dec.70
*Lieutenants.* (2)
Chas. F. Phillips, *p.*  31Dec.70
Chas. E. Longmore, *p.s.* 22July74
*2nd Lieutenant.* (1)

*A.S.* John Woodhouse    8Dec.60

---

#### Hertfordsh. *contd.*

**2nd.—*Watford.* 1 A. Bn.**
*Captain.* (1)
Alf. J. Copeland, *p.*   21Dec.72
*Lieutenants* (*lt.*1, 2nd-*lt.*1)
Geo. Edw. Lake, *p.*     25Jan.73
Chas. R. Humbert, *p,*   1June73
*Hon. A. Surg.*
Fra. Hen. Wilson Iles    23Feb.61

---

**3rd.—*St. Albans,* 1 A. Bn.**
*Captain.* (1)
Henry R. Howard, *p.*    18Jan.72
*Lieutenants* (*lt.*1, 2nd-*lt.*1)
Aubrey Kumball, *p.*     27Mar.72
Sam. M. White (*p*)      31Dec.73
*Hon. Chaplain.*
Rev. Philip U. Brown     8Apr.68
*Hon. A. Surg.*
Fredk. R. Webster       12June69

---

**4th.—*Ashridge.* 1 A. Bn.**
*Captain.* (1)
A. W. B. Earl Brownlow, *late*
Ens. & Lieut. Gr. Gds., *p.s.*
                        13June66
*Lieutenants* (*lt.*1, 2nd-*lt.*1)
Benj. Hamilton, *p.*     28Oct.63
Windsor R. Heneage, *p.* 24Dec.73

---

**5th.—*Hemel Hempstead.*
1 A. Bn.**
*Captain.* (1)
Dudley H. Ryder, *p.*    3Dec.60
*Lieutenant.* (1)
Henry Day, *p.*          12Apr.60
*2nd Lieutenant.* (1)
Charles A. Hall          15Feb.79
*Hon. A. Surg.*
Septimus B. Farr         19June61

---

**6th.—*Bishops Stortford.*
2 A. Bn.**
*Captain.* (1)
Edward Taylor, *p.*      10Nov.71
*Lieutenant.* (1)
Percy W. Taylor, *p.*    5Nov.68
*2nd Lieutenant.* (1)

---

#### Hertfordsh. *contd.*

**7th.—*Berkhampstead.*
1 A. Bn.**
*Captain.* (1)
*Lieutenants* (*lt.*1, 2nd-*lt.*1)
Edward Pope, *p.*        1May66
Henry J. Foster, *p.*    24June74
*Hon. Chaplain.*
Rev. Art. Loxley, *M.A.* 1Nov.71

---

**9th.—*Ware.* 2 A. Bn.**
*Captain.* (1)
Herbert W. Bonsor       21May79
*Lieutenant.* (1)
Geo. H. Gisby, *p.*      6Sept.73
*2nd Lieutenant.* (1)
Frederic W. Chuck       11June79
*Acting Surg.*
Henry O. F. Butcher      5Mar.79
*Acting Chaplain.*
Rev. Henry H. Coddington, *M.A.*
                        8Feb.79

---

**10th.—*Royston.* 2 A. Bn.**
*Captain.* (1)
Herbert G. Fordham, *p.* 10Jan.77
*Lieutenant.* (1)

*2nd Lieutenant.* (1)

*Acting Surg.*
Daniel B. Balding        17July78
*Acting Chaplain.*
Rev. J. Harrison, *M.A.* 23May77

---

**14th.—*Welwyn.* 2 A. Bn.**
*Captain Commandant.* (1)
Arthur M. Blake, *late* Lt. &
Capt. Gren. Gds., *p.* 13Mar.78
*Captain.* (1)
Eardley F. B. Denton     8Jan.79
*Lieutenants.* (2)
Robert C. Smith          10May79
*2nd Lieutenant.* (1)

*Acting Surg.*
John A. Kite             30Dec.76
                        1Oct.77

---

*County Rifle Volunteer Corps are listed alphabetically in a separate section of the Army List. Within
the entry for Hertfordshire the officers of the numbered corps (see Table 3.1) are shown, together with
the headquarters staff of the two administrative battalions. The following year the individual corps
were 'consolidated' (see page 22) to form the 1st and 2nd Hertfordshire Rifle Volunteer Corps, which
in turn became the 1st and 2nd Volunteer Battalions of the Bedfordshire Regiment.*

2.            June 1908

THE BEDFORDSHIRE REGIMENT—(Regtl. Dist. No. **16**)—*contd.*

## 1st (Hertfordshire) Volunteer Battalion

(1st Hertfordshire).

"South Africa, 1900-02."

[183]

Hertford.

*Hon. Colonel.*
✗Salisbury, J. E. H., Marq. of, O.B., Lt.-Col. 4Bn. Bedf. R., Col., A.D.C. (H)
    5May06

*Lt.-Colonel.*
p.s Longmore, C. E., vᴅ ⊗, hon. c. 4July00

*Majors.*
p.s Hoare, A. F., vᴅ, hon. l.c. (Q) 4Nov.93
p. Gripper, B. J., vᴅ, hon. l.c. ⊗ t.a. 25July00

*Captains.* (9)
p. Gilbertson, J. H., vᴅ, hon. m. 19Jan.89
p.s Baker, H., vᴅ, hon. m. ⊕ 18Mar.96
p.s McMullen, O. R. 25July00
p.s Christie, O. F. (H) ⊕ I. of M. 12Feb.02
p. Croft, H. P. 24Jan.03
p. Gold, C., jun. 25July03
p.s Scott-Gatty, C. C. S. (H) 2June08

*Lieuts and 2nd Lieuts.* (14)

*Lieutenants.*
p. Smith, J. H. (H) 14Oct.02
p.s Hunt, J. D. (t) 9July04
p.s ✗Page, F. (t) 9July04
p.s Phillips, E. C. M. 9July04
p.s Wilkinson, G. S. 31Mar.06
p.s Lucas, F. R. T. 31Mar.06
p.s Mitchell, H. C. B. (t) 2June06
p.s Kennedy, C. C. M. 2June06
p.s Gough, J. B. T. (t) 13Oct.06
p Pawle, J. 11July07

---

*2nd Lieutenants.*
p.s Wightman, C. F. 20Dec.05
p.s Clerk, A. G. 17Feb.06
p.s Page, E. (t) 19Mar.06
(p.s) Macpherson, R. E. (t) 11Apr.06
Glasscock, T. B. 9Mar.07
Barnes, E. C. 11May07
Boyd, A. C. (H) 20July07
Longmore, P. E. 8Feb.08

*Inst. of Musk.*
Christie, O. F., capt. 12Jan07

*Adjutant.*
✗Sworder, F. R. F., Capt.Gord.Highrs 8Feb.07
(Capt. in the Army 8Feb.07)

*Quarter-Master.*
Barber, T., hon lt. 19Aug.06

*Medical Officers.*
p. Patch, H. H. L., Surg.-Capt. 2July04
Kite, J. A., Surg.-Lt. 30Dec.76
    1Oct.77
p. Foster, A. H., Surg.-Lt. 2June06

*Acting Chaplains.*
Harrison, Rev. J., M.A. 23May77
Johnston, Rev. F.B., B.A. 26Jan.89
Crofton, Rev. W. d'A., M.A. 16Feb.89
Gainsford, Rev. G. B., M.A 24Feb.96
Baumer, Rev. L. F. 15June07
Roberts, Rev. E. K. 15Feb.08

[Scarlet. Facings—White.]

---

### Cadet Corps.

(1.)
Haileybury College.

*Captains.*
p.s Latham, P.H. (t) 1July00
    hon. 4Feb.99
p.s Reid, C. J. 14Oct.02

*2nd Lieutenant.*
Atherton, R. P. 12Feb.02
[Scarlet. Facings—White.]

(2.)
Bishop's Stortford Grammar School.
*2nd Lieutenants.*
Ingram, C. W. 28Apr.06
[Drab.]

(3.)
Hertford Grammar School
*Captain.*
p. Kinman, G. W. (H) 10Feb.06
*2nd Lieutenant.*
[Blue.]

## 2nd (Hertfordshire) Volunteer Battalion

(late 2nd Hertfordshire).

"South Africa, 1900-02."

[184]

Hemel Hempstead.

*Hon. Colonel.*
p.s Brownlow, Rt. Hon. A. W B., Earl, vᴅ, late Ens. & Lt. G Gds. Col., A.D.C. 9Mar.01

*Lt.-Colonel.*
p. Braithwaite, C. C. 16June07

*Major.*
p.s Timson, S. R., vᴅ, hon. l.c. 7May02

*Captains.* (7)
p. Jenney, S. W., vᴅ, hon. m. 21May87
p.s Parsons, J., hon. m. (C), 7Mar.00
p.s Riggall, J. K. 7May02
p.s Dwight, E. J. 7May02
p.s Jones, E. M. (Q) (H), (C), I. of M. 25Mar.05
Gallop, J. A. 1Dec.06

*Lieuts. and 2nd Lieuts.* (11)

*Lieutenants.*
p.s Stafford, W. S 22Apr.03
    20May02
(p.) Mitchell-Innes, E. A. 18Feb.05
p.s Whitworth, F. 11June.07
    22Apr 05
(p.s) Boys, S. G. 1Aug.07

*2nd Lieutenants.*
Vaisey, R. M. 1June07

*Inst. of Musk.*
Jones, E. M., capt 23Jan.04

*Adjutant.*
✗Thoyts, F. G. G., Capt. Som. L.I. 20Jan.06
(Capt. in the Army 8Mar.00)

*Quarter-Master*
p. Kirby, J. H., hon. lt. 5May06

---

*Medical Officers.*
p. Rudyard, H. A. Surg.-Capt. 27Aug.99
p. McBride, J. B., Surg.-Capt. 25Mar.05
p. Beard, T., Surg.-Capt. 2Dec.05
    21Jan.05

*Acting Chaplains.*
Gee, Rev. L. 12Dec.03

[Grey. Facings—Grey.]

---

### Cadet Corps.

[1]
Berkhampstead School

*Captain.*
p.s Parsons, J, hon. m., (Capt. and Hon. Maj. 2 V.B. Bedf. R.) 1July00
    hon. 28July97

*Lieutenant.*
Herbert, H. B. 11June02
[Grey. Facings—Dark Blue ]

[2]
St. Alban's School, Herts.

*Captain.*
p.s Jones, E. M.(H) (Q) (Capt. 2 V.B. Bedf. R.) 14Feb.03

*Lieutenant.*
Hunt, E. G. 21Nov.06

*2nd Lieutenant.*
[Drab.]

---

*The four Volunteer battalions now follow the two Regular and two Militia battalions in the section covering the Bedfordshire Regiment. Note that the battle honour awarded in recognition of the services of the volunteer active service companies (see page 45) is now shown at the top of each battalion's entry and that it is no longer possible to distinguish the sub-unit with which an officer is serving. At the time this list was published the 1st and 2nd (Hertfordshire) Volunteer Battalions were already in process of amalgamating to form the Hertfordshire Regiment and the attached cadet corps were transferring to the Officers Training Corps.*

3. **November 1914**

## THE HERTFORDSHIRE REGIMENT.

A Hart lodged, in water.

1st Bn .. .. .. .. .. Hertford.

⊗**1st Battalion.**
"South Africa, 1900-02."
*Agents*—Messrs. Holt & Co.

*Hon. Colonel*
p.s. Brownlow, Rt. Hon.
A. W. B., Earl, VD,
*late* Ens. & Lt. G
Gds., Col. A.D.C.
9Mar.01

*Lt.-Colonel*
✗Hampden, T. W.,
*Visct.* Maj. ret.
pay (*Res. of Off.*)
12Feb.13
Longmore, *Sir* C. E.,
K.C.B. (*Lt.-Col. &
Hon. Col. ret. T.F.*
28Oct.14

*Majors.*
Gripper, B. J., VD,
*hon. l.c.* ⓣ *t.a.*25July00
Baker, F.., VD,
ⓣ 7May12
Croft, H. P. 14Feb.14
p.s. Scott-Gatty, C. C. S.
(*H*) *28Oct.14
Gold, C. (*Capt. ret.
Vols.*) *28Oct.14

*Captains.*
p.s. Jones. E. M. (Q) (*H*)
25Mar.05
p.s. ✗Page, F. (*t*) 29Mar.11
p.s. Mitchell, H. C. B.
(*t*) 7Jan.12
p.s. Kennedy, C. C. M., s.
15Mar.12

*Captains*—contd.
p.s. Gough, J. B. T, (q)(*H*)
7May12
Daniel, J. C.,s. 26June13
Boyd, A. C. (*H*)
I. of M. 14Feb.14
p.s. Hunt, J.D.(*t*)Ⓢ 19Aug.14
6Apr.13
p.s. Christie, O. F. (*H*)
26Sept.14
p.s. Phillips, E. C. M.
26Sept.14
p.s. Clerk, A. G 26Sept.14
Longmore, P. E. Ⓢ
26Sept.14
Smeathman, L. F. (*H*)
26Sept.14
Pullar, F. C. *28Oct.14
Sanders, R. O. 28Oct.14
Bates, E. C. 28Oct.14
Pryor, W. M. *28Oct.14
Simonds, J. 28Oct.14
Lowry, S. H. *28Oct.14

*Lieutenants.*
p. Pawle, J 13July07
p.s. Wightman, C. F Ⓢ
1Nov.09
Pawle, H. 12Nov.13
Bevan, T. R. 19Aug.14
15Feb.14
Palmer, V. H. 26Sept.14
Times, W. O. 26Sept.14
Whitfield, G.E.26Sept.14
Brown, G. M. 26Sept.14
Snowden, H. J.
26Sept.14
Pawle, G. S. *28Oct.14
Molony, B. C. *28Oct.14
Rose, H. G. S. C.
*28Oct.14

*Lieutenants*—contd.
Pawle, F. *28Oct.14
Christie, J. F. *28Oct.14
Gibbons, T. P.*28Oct.14
Gainling, A.G.*28Oct.14

*2nd Lieutenants.*
Daish, A. J. 10July13
Bevan, J. H. 8Oct.13
Gripper, B. J. N.
12Nov.13
Le Mare, H. J. 27Feb.14
Ransom, P. L. 26Sept.14
Borwick, R. G., *late*
Lt. 20 Hrs. 26Sept.14
Milburne, B. 26Sept.14
Down, C. M. 26Sept.14
Drayson, P. 26Sept.14
Barnard, E. C. 28Oct.14
Healey,G.F.W.28Oct.14
Gold, N. P. 28Oct.14
Loyd, R. P. 28Oct.14
Gold, L. G. 28Oct.14
Oldham, R. D. 28Oct.14
Dodgson, G. 28Oct.14
Perry, D. 28Oct.14
Milne, A. R. 28Oct.14
Roberts, E. H. G.
28Oct.14

*Inst. of Musk.*
Boyd, A. C., *capt.*
14June11

*Adjutant.*
Gathorne-Hardy,
Hon. N. C., Capt.
Rif. Brig. 8Feb.12

*Quarter-Masters.*
Barber, T., TD, *hon. m.*
19Aug.06
Allen, R. R., *hon.
capt.* *28Oct.14

*Medical Officers.*
p. Rudyard, Maj. H. A.,
R.A.M.C. (T.F.)
(*attd.*) 4Aug.14
24July95
Clarke, Lt. S. H.,
M.D., R.A.M.C.
(T.F.) (*attd.*) 24Oct.14

*Chaplains.*
Crofton, *Rev.* W. d'A.
M.A., TD, Chapl. 1st
Class (T.F.) (*attd.*)
16Feb.09
16Feb.89
Gainsford,*Rev.*G.B., TD,
M.A., Chapl.3rdClass
(T.F.) (*attd.*) 1Apr.08
26Feb.96

[Uniform—Scarlet,
Facings—White.]

—————

*Cadet Units affiliated.*
2nd Hertfordshire (Watford
Scouts) Cadet Company.
3rd Hertfordshire Cadets
(Stortford School)
4th Hertfordshire Cadets
(St. George's School)
Bishop's Stortford College
Cadet Corps.

---

*The Hertfordshire Regiment now has its own entry in the section headed 'Infantry, Territorial Force', which covers the independent Territorial infantry regiments, including the London Regiment (26 battalions), the Inns of Court Officers Training Corps and the four cyclist battalions. The raising of 1st Reserve Battalion The Hertfordshire Regiment (later 2nd/1st Battalion) in the autumn of 1914 (see page 66) is apparent from the re-instatement of Sir Charles Longmore in a lieutenant-colonel's appointment and the fact that two quartermasters and two medical officers are shown. The adjutant of the new battalion has evidently yet to be appointed. Later editions of the Monthly Army List distinguish, by means of a figure 1,2,3 or 4 in front of an officer's name, the battalion with which he was serving. By December 1916 the regimental entry extended to nearly two pages of the Monthly Army List and included nearly 150 officers of the regiment serving with the four battalions or in extra-regimentally employed posts and twenty-two officers of other regiments attached to the 1st Battalion in France.*

4.                          December 1939

## THE HERTFORDSHIRE REGIMENT.

*(Forms part of the Corps of The Bedfordshire and Hertfordshire Regiment—see page* 882.)

A hart lodged, in water.

" South Africa, 1900–02."

*The Great War.*—4 *Battalions.*—" **Ypres, 1914, '17,**" " **Nonne Bosschen,**" " **Festubert, 1915,**" " **Loos,**"
" **Somme, 1916, '18,**" " **Thiepval,**" " **Ancre Heights,**" " **Ancre, 1916,**" " **Pilckem,**" " **Menin Road,**"
" **Polygon Wood,**" " **Broodseinde,**" " **Poelcappelle,**" " **Passchendaele,**" " **St. Quentin,**" " **Rosières,**" " **Lys,**"
" **Kemmel,**" " **Albert, 1918,**" " **Bapaume, 1918,**" " **Hindenburg Line,**" " **Havrincourt,**" " **Cambrai, 1918,**"
" **Selle,**" " **Sambre,**" " **France and Flanders, 1914–18.**"

Record and Pay Office      ...      ...      ...      ...      ...      *Warwick.*

| Territorial Army. | | Territorial Army—*contd.* | | Territorial Army—*contd.* | |
|---|---|---|---|---|---|
| *Hon. Colonels.* | | *Lieutenants—contd.* | | *2nd Lieutenants—contd.* | |
| H.M. THE QUEEN | | Glossop, G. C. W. | 24/8/39 | Priestley, J. F. | 24/8/39 |
| | | | 15/5/39 | | 10/5/39 |
| ✕*Hampden*, The Visct., G.C.V.O., | | | 17/2/29 | Loader, O. C. | 24/8/39 |
| K.C.B., C.M.G.(*Hon. Brig.-Gen.* | | Ottoway, J. C. | 24/8/39 | | 10/5/39 |
| *ret. T.A.) (Maj. ret. pay) t.a.* | | | 15/5/39 | Gibbs, A. A. | 24/8/39 |
| | 5/4/30 | | 1/3/30 | | 10/5/39 |
| | | Lofts, M. H. | 24/8/39 | Griffin, A. R. F. | 24/8/39 |
| *Lt.-Colonels.* | | | 18/7/39 | | 10/5/39 |
| ✕Longmore, J. A., M.B.E., T.D., | | *2nd Lieutenants.* | | Morris, A. H. | 24/8/39 |
| *t.a.* | 24/8/39 | Thomson, D. S. | 24/8/39 | | 1/6/39 |
| | 1/1/37 | | 18/7/36 | | 21/3/39 |
| ✕Sebright. *Sir* Giles E., *Bt., t.a.* | | Bone, G. | 24/8/39 | Wilson, F. | 24/8/39 |
| | 24/8/39 | | 3/3/37 | | 21/6/39 |
| | 27/5/39 | Grey, I. W. S. | 24/8/39 | Law, E. D. C. | 24/8/39 |
| | | | 24/3/37 | | 27/6/39 |
| *Majors.* | | Foljambe, P. G. W. S. | 24/8/39 | Halsey, G. M. | 24/8/39 |
| Hutcheson, A. B. | 24/8/39 | | 29/5/37 | | 28/6/39 |
| | 1/1/37 | Smith, S. C. | 24/8/39 | Wilkins, R. S. | 24/8/39 |
| | 1/1/35 | | 14/7/37 | | 28/6/39 |
| Glyn, F. M. G. | 24/8/39 | Barnett, P. C. | 24/8/39 | Pryor, J. M. | 24/8/39 |
| | 30/6/39 | | 5/1/38 | | 1/7/39 |
| Malcolmson, B. J. F., *t.s.c.* | 24/8/39 | Hodgson, E. S. | 24/8/39 | Walker, T. G. A. | 29/7/39 |
| | 1/7/39 | | 4/5/38 | | 8/7/39 |
| *Captains.* | | Smith, H. A. V. | 24/8/39 | Tuckey, H. L. | 24/8/39 |
| Christie, P. N. | 24/8/39 | | 19/7/38 | | 8/7/39 |
| | 1/4/37 | Pilkington, C. L. | 24/8/39 | Cook, P. H. | 24/8/39 |
| McMullen, R. P., M.B.E. | 24/8/39 | | 28/7/38 | | 8/7/39 |
| | 9/11/38 | Mitchell, R. E. | 24/8/39 | Slenieck, D. C. | 24/8/39 |
| Lindesell, J. C. | 24/8/39 | | 18/1/39 | | 8/7/39 |
| | 1/4/39 | Humbert, R. A. | 24/8/39 | Jarrett, A. F. R. | 24/8/39 |
| Passingham, B. | 24/8/39 | | 18/1/39 | | 29/7/39 |
| | 15/5/39 | Parsons, C. H. J. | 24/8/39 | Cole, C. B. | 24/8/39 |
| | 14/10/31 | | 18/1/39 | | 2/9/39 |
| Thomson, G. E. | 24/8/39 | Burnett-Stuart, A. M. | 24/8/39 | | |
| | 1/7/39 | | 22/2/39 | *Adjutants.* | |
| | | Brand, D. F. | 24/8/39 | Norcock, R., Capt. Bedfs. & | |
| *Lieutenants.* | | | 19/4/39 | Herts. R. | 1/1/39 |
| Melville, A. D. | 24/8/39 | Nicols, W. R. | 24/8/39 | Andrews, Capt. (*Actg.*) A. Bedfs. | |
| | 4/4/37 | | 10/5/39 | & Herts. R. (*temp.*) | 23/4/39 |
| Richardson, R. C. (*A/Capt.* | | Gold, C. C. | 24/8/39 | | |
| 1/9/39) *s.* | 24/8/39 | | 10/5/39 | *Quarter-Masters.* | |
| | 17/11/37 | Robinson, M. R. L. | 24/8/39 | ✕Gibson, S. C., *lt.* | 24/8/39 |
| Sheppard, G. H. (*A/Capt.* 4/9/39) | | | 10/5/39 | | 1/6/39 |
| | 24/8/39 | Lyon, *Hon.* D. B. | 24/8/39 | ✕Sandys, W. F., *lt.* | 24/8/39 |
| | 13/4/38 | | 10/5/39 | | 17/8/39 |
| Burr, S. R. W. | 24/8/39 | Oliver, J. F. | 24/8/39 | | |
| | 8/6/38 | | 10/5/39 | Cadet Unit affiliated. | |
| Kenyon, G. V. | 24/8/39 | Rothwell, R. F. | 24/8/39 | 9th Herts. C. Unit. | |
| | 5/10/38 | | 10/5/39 | | |

*The Hertfordshire Regiment continues to be included in the section headed 'Infantry-Territorial Army'.
Note the inclusion of the regiments battle honours for the First World War (known officially as 'The
Great War') and the entry showing that Her Majesty The Queen is now Honorary Colonel. It is again
apparent from the double entries for lieutenant-colonels, adjutants and quartermasters that two
battalions are in existence. Officers were not commissioned into the Territorial Army during the Second
World War, so this extract lists all those who were on the active list of the regiment at the outbreak
of war. (Officers on the Territorial Army Reserve of Officers list were shown separately.) The date
24.8.39 beside each officer's name represents the date on which all Territorial officers were deemed to
have been embodied, regardless of the date they actually reported for duty.*

# Bibliography

ARMITAGE, A. 'The Hertfordshire Guards of 1914' *Hertfordshire Countryside*, Vol. XXII, No. 109, May 1968.

BAKER, H. *The Territorial Force – A Manual of its Law, Organisation and Administration*, London, John Murray, 1909.

BARNETT, C. *Britain and Her Army 1509–1970 – A Military, Political and Social Survey*, London, Alan Lane (The Penguin Press), 1970.

BARTHORP, M. *Crater to Creggan – The History of the Royal Anglian Regiment 1964–1974*, London, Leo Cooper Ltd., 1976.

BECKE, A. F. *Order of Battle of Divisions 1914–1918*, (6 Vols.) London, His Majesty's Stationery Office, 1934–1945.

BECKETT, I. F. W. *Riflemen Form – A Study of the Rifle Volunteer Movement 1859–1908*, Aldershot, The Ogilby Trusts, 1982.

BERRY, R. P. *A History of the Formation and Development of the Volunteer Infantry . . .* London, Simpkin Marshall and Co. Ltd., 1903.

BLAXLAND, G. *The Regiments Depart – A History of the British Army 1945–1970* London, William Kimber and Co. Ltd., 1971.

BRIDGEMAN, C. *Quick and Slow Marches for the Hertfordshire Volunteer Associations*, 1800 [British Library].

BROCK, A. St. H. *7th Hertfordshire Battalion Home Guard – A History of the Battalion, 1940–1944*, Berkhamsted, Hertfordshire, Clunbury Press (Printers), 1945.

BUSBY, J. H. 'Local Military Forces in Hertfordshire 1793–1814' *Journal of the Society for Army Historical Research*, Vol XXXI, No. 125, Spring 1953.

COUSINS, G. *The Defenders – A History of the British Volunteer*, London, Frederick Muller Ltd., 1968.

CREAGH, Sir O'M and HUMPHRIS E. M. *The V.C. and the D.S.O.*, London, Standard Art Book Company, n.d., Vol. 1., pp. 310–311.

CROFT, H. P. 1st Baron *My Life of Strife*, London, Hutchinson and Co. Ltd., n.d. [c. 1947].

CUNNINGHAM, H. *The Volunteer Force – A Social and Political History 1859–1908*, London, Croom Helm Ltd., 1975.

DUNLOP, J. K. *The Development of the British Army 1899–1914*, London, Methuen and Co., 1938.

DUNLOP, J. K., *The Territorial Army Today*, London, A. and C. Black, 1939.

'C.F.D.' *Salute to the Hertfordshire Regiment*, Hertford Borough and Rural District National Savings Committee, 1944.

EDMONDS, J. E. *History of the Great War: Military Operations – France and Belgium 1914–18*, (14 Vols. + Maps, etc.) London, Macmillan and Co. Ltd., 1925–1939.

EVANS, E. T. *Records of the Third Middlesex Rifle Volunteers*, London, Simpkin, Marshall and Co., 1885.

FELLOWS, R. B. *Historical Records of the Hertfordshire Militia to 1892*, St. Albans, Gibbs and Bamforth, 1893.

FORTESCUE, Hon. J. W. *The County Lieutenancies and the Army 1803–1814*, London, Macmillan and Co. Ltd., 1909.

FREDERICK, J. B. M. *The Lineage Book of British Land Forces 1660–1978*, (2 Vols.) Wakefield, Yorkshire, Microform Academic Publishers, 1986.

GRAVES, C. *The Home Guard of Britain*, London, Hutchinson and Co. Ltd., 1943.

HAMILTON, C. 'A Memorable Day for the County Regiment', *Hertfordshire Countryside*, Vol. IX, No. 34, Autumn 1954, p. 66. [Report of laying up of Old Colours of 1st Battalion The Hertfordshire Regiment and ceremony of conferring the freedom of the Borough of Hertford on the Battalion – 16th May 1954].

HAY, G. J. *An Epitomised History of the Militia . . .*, London, United Services Gazette, 1905.

HINE, R. L. 'Hitchin and the threatened invasion of 1803', *Relics of an Uncommon Attorney*, London, J. M. Dent and Sons Ltd., 1951, pp. 102–114.

JAMES, E. A. *British Regiments 1914–1918*, London, Samson Books Ltd., 1978.

JERROLD, D. *The Royal Naval Division*, London, Hutchinson and Co., 1923 (Second Edition, 1927).

JOSLEN, H. F. *Orders of Battle 1939–45*, (2 Vols.), London, Her Majesty's Stationery Office, 1966.

KING, E. J. *The History of the 7th Battalion Middlesex Regiment*, London, Harrison and Sons Ltd., 1927.

KINGSFORD, C. L. *The Story of The Duke of Cambridge's Own (Middlesex Regiment)*, London, Country Life, 1916.

KNEE, H. J. 'How the Regimental Colours were brought back to Hertford', *Hertfordshire Countryside*, Vol. XXVIII, No. 170, June 1973.

MAURICE, Sir F. *The 16th Foot – A History of the Bedfordshire and Hertfordshire Regiment*, London, Constable and Co. Ltd., 1931.

MOORE, C. 'Evidence of Literacy from the Muster Roll of the Hitchin Volunteer Corps of 1803–09', *Hertfordshire's Past*, No. 2, Spring 1977.

MYATT, F. *The Royal Berkshire Regiment (The 49th/66th Regiment of Foot)*, London, Hamish Hamilton Ltd., 1968.

NEALE, D. H. *9th Hertfordshire Battalion Home Guard – A History 1940–1945*, Watford, Sun Engraving Co. Ltd. (Printers), 1946.

ORGILL, D. *The Gothic Line*, London, Wm. Heinemann Ltd., 1967.

PAGE, W. E. 'With the famous 1st Hertfordshires in the front line', *Hertfordshire Countryside*, Vol. XXIV, No. 125, September 1969.

PETERS, G. W. H. *The Bedfordshire and Hertfordshire Regiment*, London, Leo Cooper Ltd., 1970.

PETRE, F. L. *The Royal Berkshire Regiment (Princess Charlotte of Wales's) 49th–66th Foot*, (2 Vols.) Reading, 1925.

PIGRAM, R. J. 'Boney's Bogies – A Review of the Hitchin Volunteers', *Hertfordshire Countryside*, Vol. XXIII and XXIV, Nos. 121 and 122, May and June 1969.

RICHARDS, W. *His Majesty's Territorial Army*, (4 Vols.) London, Virtue and Co., n.d. [c. 1910].

SAINSBURY, J. D. *Hertfordshire's Soldiers from 1757*, Hitchin, Hertfordshire, Hertfordshire Local History Council, 1969.

SAINSBURY, J. D. 'Uniform and Badges of the Hertfordshire Volunteer Regiment 1914–1919', *Hertfordshire Past and Present*, No. 13, 1973.

SAINSBURY, J. D. *A Guide to the History of the Bedfordshire and Hertfordshire Regiment*, Digswell, Hertfordshire, Hart Books, 1987.

SALISBURY, J. C. 1st Marquess of, *A Narrative of the Preparations made at Hatfield for their Majesties and the Royal Family to review the Volunteer Corps of the County of Hartford, Friday 13th June 1800*, Hatfield, 1800.

SEBAG–MONTEFIORE, G. *A History of the Volunteer Forces from the Earliest Times to the Year 1860*, London, Constable and Co. Ltd., 1908.

SELLWOOD, A. V. *The Saturday Night Soldiers – The Stirring Story of the Territorial Army*, London, White Lion Publishers Ltd., 1974 (2nd Edition).

STANHOPE, H. *The Soldiers – An Anatomy of the British Army*, London, Hamish Hamilton Ltd., 1979.

WALLACE, E. *Kitchener's Army and the Territorial Forces*, London, George Newnes Ltd., n.d. [1915].

WEBSTER, F. A. M. *A History of the 5th Battalion The Bedfordshire and Hertfordshire Regiment (T.A.)*, London, F. Warne and Co. Ltd., 1930.

WESTERN, J. R. *The English Militia in the Eighteenth Century*, London, Routledge and Kegan Paul, 1965.

WESTLAKE, R. A. *The Rifle Volunteers 1859–1908*, Chippenham, Wiltshire, Picton Publishing, 1982.

WESTLAKE, R. A. *The Territorial Battalions – A Pictorial History*, Tunbridge Wells, Kent, Spellmount Ltd., 1986.

WILLSON, J. *A view of the Volunteer Army of Great Britain in the Year 1806 . . .* (Brief details of uniforms; also available in J.S.A.H.R., Vol. XXXI, No. 127, Autumn 1953).

WILSON, R. D. *'Cordon and Search' – With 6th Airborne Division in Palestine*, Aldershot, Hampshire, Gale and Polden Ltd., 1949.

Wood, E. *et al.*, *The Citizen Soldier – An Authoritative Account of the Training and Duties of the Territorial Army . . .*, London, Hutchinson and Co. Ltd., n.d. [1939].

Wroughton, J. B. *A Short Account of the 1st (Hertfordshire) Volunteer Battalion The Bedfordshire Regiment in South Africa*, Hertford, Stephen Austin and Sons Ltd. (Printers), 1905.

Wyrall, E. *The History of the Second Division 1914–18* London, T. Nelson and Sons, 1921.

Wyrall, E. *The Die-Hards in the Great War . . .*, (2 Vols.) London, Harrison and Sons Ltd., 1926–30.


1st Infantry Division *History of the First Division – Florence to Monte Grande August 1944–January 1945*, Cairo, Schindler's Press, n.d.

1st Battalion The Bedfordshire and Hertfordshire Regiment *Presentation of New Colours to 1st Battalion The Bedfordshire and Hertfordshire Regiment*, (Souvenir programme with coloured plate of new colours. For illustrated account of the ceremony see *The Wasp and The Eagle*, Vol. II, No. 2, December 1963.)

1st Battalion The Bedfordshire and Hertfordshire Regiment 'Regimental History' [Typescript, duplicated] Hertford, 1963.

1st (Hertfordshire) Volunteer Battalion The Bedfordshire Regiment *Standing Orders*, Hertford, Stephen Austin and Sons Ltd., 1906.

1st Battalion The Hertfordshire Regiment *List of Officers, Warrant Officers, N.C.O.s, and Other Ranks who were killed in action or died of wounds or sickness contracted on active service abroad in the Great War*, Hertford, 1920.

1st Battalion The Hertfordshire Regiment *Standing Orders*, Hertford, 1934.

1st Battalion The Hertfordshire Regiment *Hertfordshire Field Gazette: Italian Campaign August 1944 – January 1945*, [Palestine] 1945.

1st Battalion The Hertfordshire Regiment *A Short History of the Hertfordshire Regiment*, Aldershot, Hampshire, Gale and Polden Ltd., n.d. [1950].

1st Battalion The Hertfordshire Regiment *Presentation of New Colours to the 1st Battalion The Hertfordshire Regiment and the 5th Battalion The Bedfordshire and Hertfordshire Regiment*, Hertford, 1953 (Souvenir programme with order of ceremony and coloured plate of new colours. For an illustrated account of the ceremony see *The Wasp*, Vol. XIV, No. 3, December 1953.)

1st Battalion The Hertfordshire Regiment *Form and Order of Service for the laying up of the Old Colours 16th May 1954*, Hertford, 1954. (For an illustrated account of the ceremony see *The Wasp* Vol. XIV, No. 5, August 1954.)

'The Colours of the Hertfordshire Regiment', *Hertfordshire Countryside*, Vol. IX, No. 35, Winter 1954–55.

*Officers Died in the Great War 1914–1919*, London, His Majesty's Stationery Office, 1919.

*Soldiers Died in the Great War 1914–1919, Part 21 – The Bedfordshire and Hertfordshire Regiment*, London, His Majesty's Stationery Office, 1921.

*Soldiers died in the Great War 1914–1919, Part 77 – The Hertfordshire Regiment*, London, His Majesty's Stationery Office, 1921.

*The Territorial Year Book – 1909*, London, Hodder and Stoughton, 1909.

*The Territorial and Auxiliary Forces of Hertfordshire*, London, Reid-Hamilton Ltd., n.d. [1950] pp., 39–48.

**Regimental Magazines**

The Bedfordshire and Hertfordshire Regiment *The Wasp* 1922–1958
The 3rd East Anglian Regiment *The Wasp and the Eagle* 1959–1964
The Royal Anglian Regiment *The Castle* 1965–
4th Battalion The Bedfordshire Regiment *The Hart – Regimental Journal of the Hertford-shire Militia* 1903 and 1904 (two numbers only published).

Local history librarians of the main branches of Hertfordshire County Library will be able to advise on the availability of these magazines in Hertfordshire and Bedfordshire. Substantial, but not necessarily complete, runs of *The Wasp* are also held at the Imperial War Museum, The National Army Museum and Hertford Museum.

**Official Publications**

*London Gazette*
*Army Lists*, especially the *Monthly Army List*
*General Orders* (later *Army Orders*)
*Auxiliary and Reserve Forces Circulars*
*Army Council Instructions* (now *Defence Council Instructions – Army*)

The *London Gazette* is registered as a newspaper and is held by a number of major public reference libraries.

Details of the various *Army Lists* and lists covering the Auxiliary Forces are given in WHITE, A. S. 'The Army List' *Journal of the Society for Army Historical Research*, Vol. XXV, No. 103, Autumn 1947 and Vol. XLV, No. 181, Spring 1967. *Army Lists*, together with the *Orders, Circulars* and *Instructions* mentioned above, are published by H.M.S.O. for the War Office (now Ministry of Defence) and on publication were subject to varying degrees of security classiciation, and hence availability. In general, these security classifications have now been removed and such copies as have reached public reference libraries are available without restriction. Readers requiring advice on these specialised sources are recommended to consult the National Army Museum (Department of Records).